MARRIAGE WITHOUT THE SEX

MARRIAGE WITHOUT THE SEX

AN UNCONVENTIONAL APPROACH
TO BUSINESS RELATIONSHIPS

RACHEL SCHAFFER LAWSON

MARRIAGE WITHOUT THE SEX

An Unconventional Approach to Business Relationships

ISBN   978-1-61961-760-5 *Hardcover*

978-1-61961-761-2 *Paperback*

978-1-61961-762-9 *Ebook*

To Tyler, my partner in life, ride or die.

CONTENTS

———

FOREWORD

BY PATRICIA A. SCHAFFER

———

I am writing the foreword to this book as someone who knows this author better than anyone in this world: her mother. The book touched me in many ways, both personally and professionally. I felt something, and I learned something, which, quite frankly, happens less and less in this stage of my life. To say I am proud of my girl and the accomplished woman she has become is an understatement. This endeavor just adds to her many other achievements over the past thirty-three years. You go girl! I love you more than words can say.

Now, I'd like to say a few words about the book. Oftentimes

in management courses or how-to books, the emphasis is mainly on rules, laws, processes, and procedures—not on the human side of the equation. This book adds that human dimension of forming and operating a business to the mix. Interpersonal communication is rarely considered at the outset of the relationship, but it is vitally important in its success. In forming my first business over twenty years ago, I did not fully understand that concept. Lack of communication was a major contributing factor in its failure. Rachel lived through that time of life with me. She learned from my mistakes.

I think this book will be helpful to people who are starting their own businesses, and it will give them reason to pause and fully assess if and how they should proceed. Forming a business with someone is not something to be rushed into without thinking through the concepts and points illustrated in this book. Through the real-life examples and situations presented here, it is easy to understand the points to consider during the process. It is food for thought, and it is critical to success.

In summary, this book would have greatly benefited me twenty years ago. It would have saved me years of pain and suffering when I blindly stumbled into a business relationship with little thought about what would happen if it didn't work out. I didn't have a partnership agreement, my partner and I did not clearly define our business roles, and we had very different opinions on many small and eventually large business decisions. I grew to resent my partner and no longer trusted him in our business relationship.

This book could have changed the course of my life.

PATRICIA A. SCHAFFER

PROUD MOM OF THE AUTHOR RACHEL
SCHAFFER LAWSON AND PRESIDENT,
TOTAL QUALITY ASSOCIATES, INC.

INTRODUCTION

———

My mother once built a company from the ground up, then gave it all away.

She didn't want to. My mother is a planner. She doesn't make any move without planning every aspect of it. She studied computer programming in the 1970s, when computers barely even existed. She became an expert in data warehousing management, then spent years building database solutions for major corporations like GE, Lockheed Martin, and Oracle before deciding to strike out on her own.

She left Oracle and formed a new company in partnership with a former coworker and friend. He was very charismatic, and they had known each other for a few years before deciding to go into business together. They formed their own IT consulting business and became 50/50 partners.

Things worked well for almost a decade. He mainly concentrated on business development, and she worked on executing projects. The business was very successful and grew quickly. The company grew from just the two of them and a couple of consultants to twelve employees and several subcontractors.

I was in my first year of law school at Loyola University New Orleans when things started to unravel. Throughout most of their partnership, he had overseen the financials and she had simply trusted him and concentrated on her work. I remember being outside my apartment in New Orleans when she phoned to tell me she had looked at the books for the first time. What she saw shocked her.

She discovered a huge disparity in the amount of money each of them was bringing into the business. She was supporting most of the company financially on her shoulders alone. While she was working eighty-hour weeks, he was out on the golf course and planning basketball tournaments.

Since they'd become profitable, her business partner had

unilaterally decided it was time to put things in cruise control. He essentially lost interest in the company, leaving her to do most of the work. Then he started making hiring and purchasing decisions without her. This was the straw that broke the camel's back.

She was angry. Really angry. She decided it was time to part ways, and from there, things started to get uncomfortable. In fact, things got downright contentious.

MY MOTHER'S MISTAKE

On the face of it, my mother did everything right. She went into business with someone she knew and trusted. They had worked together for a long time and had an established relationship. They knew each other's work styles and what the other was bringing to the table. They built a profitable business together.

On paper the business was killing it, but despite being a habitual planner, my mother made a crucial mistake: she never signed any sort of partnership agreement. She and her partner didn't consult an attorney when they formed their corporation. Instead, they did all the legal work themselves. Although they brought on a corporate attorney later, this attorney represented the corporation—not the partners' individual interests.

To part ways, my mother retained her own lawyer, as did her partner. Initially, things seemed straightforward: They would split the company 50/50. She would take her projects, and he would take his. They had their company valued by a specialist.

Later, she told me, "I had this number in my head and I'm thinking, *This is great. That'll allow me to start a new company*."

That is not what happened. What happened is that her partner changed his mind and decided he wanted *everything*.

What followed was nine months of complete agony. Ugly back-and-forth fighting wore her down to the point where we worried she might have a nervous breakdown. At one point, my mother and her partner seemingly reached an agreement, only to have him back out at the last minute.

"I can imagine what divorce is like," she told me. "It probably feels the same way. In the end, I just wanted out. It wasn't worth the fight anymore."

Ultimately, she gave every single dime of the company away. She retained nothing but two of her most valued employees who followed her to her next business. It was worth it to her to end the acrimony and move on with her life.

If they had signed a partnership agreement at the beginning of their business relationship, the terms of their separation would have been outlined long before. It probably would not have taken so long to unwind from each other, and the terms would have been fairer.

Fast-forward to today. My mother is fine. More than fine—she is thriving. She formed a new company that focuses solely on data management, which is her primary interest. Her current business makes more than three times what her last one did. She is the sole owner.

She does not see or speak to her former partner. My mother doesn't at all regret her decision to cut her losses.

"Life is too short to be so miserable, and the longer I was with him, the less time I had to create something new for myself."

It was hard to watch my mother go through this, and I also felt the betrayal acutely. This guy was a family friend, we celebrated holidays with him, and he still had no problem screwing her over.

When I became an attorney and started doing my own work with business partnerships, the magnitude of her decisions really hit me. From my legal vantage point, I could really see the damage caused by jumping into a partnership unprepared. I now know there is a much better way to handle things. It starts from the moment you and your future business partner meet.

MARRIAGE AND BUSINESS

When my husband Tyler and I were getting married, we did some light premarital counseling with my rabbi. We each filled out a questionnaire on our own, then came together to talk about it later.

I mentioned this to a client one day, and he suggested I read a book called *His Needs, Her Needs: Building an Affair-Proof Marriage* by Willard F. Harley, Jr. I'm not really into relationship self-help books, but I decided to pick it up for kicks.

The premise of the book is that all human beings have the same ten needs, but how they prioritize them differs depending on their gender. Basically, men's priority is sex, and women's priority is...not sex.

Every night I would read this book aloud to my future husband. Each chapter started with a little story of two people. One spouse wasn't fulfilling the other's needs, so the injured party went off and had an affair. Seriously, every single one led to an affair.

We made it as far as chapter 5, "Conversation." I read this chapter one night and got to a section on disrespect, which is one of the enemies of intimate conversation. Halfway through, I made a side comment (I can't even remember what it was), and suddenly Tyler and I were having an enormous fight—a real barn burner. The fight lasted so long, I was exhausted. I really needed to get some sleep, but we were still fighting, and we had made a promise to each other early on to never go to bed angry.

That was the end of us reading aloud. The receipt from the bookstore is still in the book, marking the spot where we stopped to have the fight. Although I never finished the book, I continued to think about the self-help genre, which walks a fine line between providing entertainment and genuine advice.

Around the same time, I was contemplating the many similarities between romantic relationships and business relationships. They are very much alike. One day in my office, it came to me like a lightning strike: Business partnerships are literally marriages without the sex.

That's when the idea of this book started coming together. I wanted to explore the parallels between these two very important kinds of relationships in a format that would be useful to prospective business partners, but I did not want it to be as dry as most business books. Basically, this book would be a self-help guide for your business relationships.

A BOUNCING BABY BUSINESS

Good attorneys have very intimate relationships with their clients. In my mind, it's no different than a doctor-patient relationship, or a relationship with a spiritual advisor.

Client confidentiality leads to all kinds of admissions. I bet if you asked people if they are more honest with their doctor or their lawyer, an overwhelming number would say their lawyer. After all, how many people admit to their doctor that they've done drugs? Significantly fewer than apparently feel comfortable telling me about it.

In my practice, I become very close with clients, and we develop long-term relationships. They often feel they can open up and tell me their deep, dark secrets. Sometimes they need to so I can do my job effectively. There comes a point when I feel more like a therapist than a legal advisor. The conversations tend to go like this: "I'm sorry that things aren't going well with you and your business partner. Have you tried talking to each other? Are you really *hearing* what they are saying?"

I get really involved in the relationships between partners, and then we create something new: a business. When my clients start a new company, I like to say, "Congratulations, you've just popped out a baby. You're a mom now—or one of those male seahorses that give birth."

You've birthed a child. This baby is now dependent on you for everything. That's a lot of responsibility. If you and your partner start fighting, what's going to happen to that baby?

In this scenario, I'm basically the social worker. I'm coming in to act on behalf of the child who can't speak for itself. A business doesn't have a voice; it speaks through me. As the company's attorney, I can sue one of the parents if they do something to hurt the business.

That's a heavy load, which is why it's important to have a long, well-reasoned conversation about starting a business together—just like you would about having an actual baby.

FOR ME, IT'S PERSONAL

People are so excited when they first come to me with the intent of starting a business. They're holding hands, and they are deep in business love. You can see it in their eyes. Instead of little hearts passing between them, it's little dollar signs. It's adorable. They have so many ideas and can't wait to get their business off the ground. They think everything will be perfect.

I don't just help with corporate formation (birthing the baby, if you will). I do a lot of other things too. I help protect the name or any other intellectual property the business might have, I help set up the commercial space (your business's home), and I help with contracts. I get very involved and am a patron at many of the businesses I work with. I don't want to say I'm just as invested as the owners are, but I'm damn close.

So, when people come to me and tell me they need a business divorce, it saddens me. When businesses fail, I always wonder if there was something I could have done to better prepare my clients. Did I help them end things as amicably as possible? I feel my clients' joys and pains right alongside them. They don't teach you that in law school.

HELP ME HELP YOU

You meet somebody. You spend some time with them, get to know them, find out what they are all about. You decide to enter a more formal type of relationship with them. You decide to spend your life with them and to intertwine your finances. You decide whether or not to have a child. Hopefully, you live happily ever after.

Why should a business relationship be any different? My goal for this book is to encourage people to take a step back. Is this relationship a good idea? Do you want to spend the rest of your life with this person? Seriously. Look at each other and tell me if you think you can spend the next forty or fifty years together.

If you don't take the time to establish a healthy relationship, you are setting yourself up for a world of hurt. I want to help you avoid the terrible situation that my mother found herself in and that some of my clients have experienced. I've seen clients lose everything they've built and start over from zero. It's crushing—just as devastating as a divorce.

If you're considering entering a partnership and use this book to build a healthy foundation, you will have a stronger, more profitable business. Or, perhaps you'll discover that the person you thought was right for you isn't and decide not to proceed. That's a win, too.

There's no one right way to have a good marriage, and there's no one right way to form a partnership. Ideally, you'll do all your groundwork before you birth the baby business. Realistically, some people don't get around to this until their business is a toddler or even a teenager. If you're already committed to your business relationship, this book is also for you. Maybe you already have a partner and are experiencing issues. This book can help you put the steps in place to get back on track and save your relationship. If you have a solid partnership, then you'll have a happier life and a better business, and you're going to make more money.

And in the end, that's what everyone wants, right?

CHAPTER 1

MEET CUTE

Nashville's Network at Night events were *the* place to connect with up-and-coming movers and shakers in the city's small business community. *Or, at least, they were supposed to be*, thought Larissa as she idly sipped her drink.

She had been trapped in a one-sided conversation with a frat-boy type in khakis for what felt like hours. As he began to mansplain the idea of crowdfunding to her, she desperately searched the bar behind him, looking for a plausible reason to excuse herself.

Maybe I should just call it a night, she thought.

She'd come out hoping to make a real connection. For

months, she'd been looking for that special someone who would truly get what a catch she was. She'd paid her dues and racked up years of industry experience managing bars around East Nashville. Now she was ready to take the next step—she just couldn't do it alone.

She locked eyes with a tall, dark stranger across the room. He had that buttoned-up financial guy look, but a rakish smile that said he also knew how to have a good time. His name was written in Sharpie on a flimsy nametag: Lance.

He strode across the bar to Larissa and introduced himself. Lance was a self-made man. He was tired of working the uptight world of corporate finance, and now he finally had the monetary means to realize his dream: He wanted to own a bar.

Before they knew it, an hour had passed. The bar started to empty out, and the staff began to wipe down the counters, but still Lance and Larissa talked excitedly. Their dreams were startlingly similar: To open a small, neighborhood craft-cocktail bar featuring locally sourced, seasonal ingredients.

"You know," said Lance, "you have the hospitality background, and I have the startup capital. This could be the beginning of a beautiful business."

Larissa blushed.

They exchanged numbers and a quick, awkward hug before agreeing to meet next weekend at Panera to talk over their ideas in more detail.

"I'm really excited," Lance gushed.

As she gathered her things to leave, Larissa noticed a slightly bent business card tucked under an empty martini glass. It read, "Rachel Schaffer Lawson, Attorney and Entrepreneur."

She picked the card up and tucked it in her pocket. It might not be a bad idea to get a lawyer's opinion on things before proceeding.

LOVE AT FIRST SIGHT? NOT SO FAST

Ah, business love! I see it every day. Couples come into my office, excited to start a business together. They have the million-dollar idea or product that is going to sell itself, and they are the dream team. There has never been, nor will there ever be, more *perfect* people to run this business.

While all might seem bright and shiny for Lance and Larissa, they face a serious uphill battle. If Larissa were to come see me, I would knock the stars out of her eyes—*fast*.

New businesses fail at an alarming rate. According to the Small Business Administration (SBA), 50 percent of businesses fail during the first year. That's even higher than the divorce rate for the first year of marriage in America! Between 2007 and 2010, failure rates for small businesses rose by 40 percent.

Business partnerships face their own set of challenges. People who go into partnerships haphazardly and without the proper planning face a failure rate of up to 80 percent.

It's not all bleak, though. Companies that do their due diligence and take a structured approach to establishing partnerships reach a success rate of up to 80 percent.

Additionally, according to the SBA, companies with multiple owners have a longer survival rate than sole proprietorships, and the individuals involved make more money on average. In many ways, two heads really are better than one.

Basically, when a business relationship is good, it's really good. When it's bad, it's really bad.

WHY IT'S SO HARD TO MAKE IT WORK

The reasons business partnerships fail are actually quite

similar to the reasons most marriages fail. Let's break these reasons down:

FINANCIAL ISSUES

Financial issues are a killer for both marriages and business partnerships. It's easy to be partners when things are going well, but when a business falls on hard times, stress levels skyrocket. Often partners find they can't take the heat or deal with the stress of building a business during lean times.

On the flip side, it's like the Notorious B.I.G. song "Mo Money Mo Problems." Becoming successful can, and very often does, lead to contention. As your business grows and changes, allocation of funds can be a major sticking point. If you've got one spender and one saver, you have a recipe for serious friction down the line.

One thing I've learned over the years is that everybody thinks other people handle money the same way they do. It's easy to assume you are on the same page when it comes to financial decisions, only to come to an ugly realization later.

Consider the following with your partner: Are you someone who wants to reinvest in the business? Or are you someone who wants to throw money at marketing or buying up inventory? Are you a spender? A saver? An investor?

COMMUNICATION PROBLEMS

Communication problems are frequent relationship killers that often go hand-in-hand with financial issues. Ironically, communication can be a contentious subject to even talk about.

If you don't begin your partnership with solid communication about your goals and values, you are cruising towards disaster. A solid foundation depends on you and your partner being on the same page about the future of your business. You also need to develop a solid understanding of the other person's communication style and tactics for conflict resolution.

PERSONALITY CLASH

As in a marriage, a business partnership functions best with complementary personalities and values. At a bare minimum, you must get along with the person you're working with.

At the same time, opposites attract. Sharing the same set of attributes doesn't necessarily make for a good partnership. It's better to have one visionary and one practical person, or one person with industry background and one with a financial background. Having complementary skill sets is one of the biggest traits I see in my successful clients.

"SEX PROBLEMS"

You are probably not having sex with your business partner, but we can equate problems in the bedroom with emotional problems in the business. Someone isn't pulling their weight, and the other person is stuck doing all the work and dragging the less enthusiastic partner along. This can lead to resentment, which is absolute poison in any kind of relationship. If you don't address resentment, it will grow and grow until it kills everything it touches.

WHO ARE YOU GETTING INTO BED WITH?

Whenever I meet with a new client and the word "partnership" comes up, I have an almost Pavlovian response. I am the nosy mother digging into their business after a date. "What's his name? What does she do? What are his intentions?" I want to know everything.

This isn't just snooping. There is a whole line of questioning we need to do to determine if two people are a good match to work together.

I might start a consultation with one partner, but I expect to sit down with both partners eventually. I want to get to know who each of them are. How did they meet? How did they come to the decision to start a business together? Why now? If they've known each other for a couple of years, they probably have the advantage of knowing more than just surface-level information about each other.

I also want to know what each of them brings to the table. In our Lance and Larissa situation, we've got Larissa bringing the industry knowledge and know-how and Lance bringing the financial backing. That's great—you need both of those things to make a business work.

Some people may come in ready to go with a fully fleshed-out business plan, while others may only have an idea to start with. But the money aspect is crucial. Sometimes people come to me with crazy, wonderful ideas, but they have absolutely no way to pay for them. We must then figure out that piece of the puzzle too, whether it's getting loans, investors, or another business partner.

RED FLAGS

Lance and Larissa would immediately raise one major red flag for me: They've just met.

I oftentimes see people who meet at networking events or are social acquaintances and decide to just jump into the business bed together. Let's think about that. This means that you are staking your financial success and livelihood on somebody you barely even know. Your finances—how you live, eat, and put a roof over your head—are dependent on a relative stranger.

When you enter a romantic relationship with someone, you might date for a while, get to know each other, then maybe decide to take the next steps towards marriage and kids. Or, you might decide this is not who you want to spend the rest of your life with and move on. Most people don't just go to Vegas and have a shotgun wedding with some person they met at a bar. No—they spend time, invest resources, and really get to know the person they might spend the rest of their life.

Yet I meet people all the time who tell me, "I met this person at an event, and we started a business six weeks later." You're telling me that you are going to tie your financial stability to someone you just met six weeks ago? Why? If we all do due diligence on our spouses, why on earth are we not doing the same with potential business partners with whom we also hope to have long, fruitful relationships?

This isn't to say a short relationship is a deal breaker. It isn't necessarily a great idea to go into business with your best friend, lover, or mother either. As John D. Rockefeller said, "A friendship founded on business is a good deal better than a business founded on friendship." No matter who you are working with, you have some work to do before you tie the knot.

SETTING EXPECTATIONS

Now it's time to talk about the business itself. Generally, both parties agree they want to start a business, but we will really dig in to determine whether they want to start the *same* business with the same value proposition. We want to make sure they both hold the same values and dreams for the business.

Anybody can start a bar, but what's the name of the bar? Where will it be? What's it going to look like? What's it going to feel like? What kind of food and drinks will it serve? There are a lot of decisions that need to be made together; just agreeing to open a bar barely scratches the surface of the situation.

One of the most important things to go over is what everybody's roles or job descriptions are going to look like. You can't just say, "We want to start this bar. We'll figure out the details later." You need to have the conversation now.

If you don't, a couple of different things could happen. Important things could fall through the cracks. Every business functions in a similar way at its core: There are financials (accounting and bookkeeping), legal, marketing, and operations. Who is going to handle each of these key pieces?

On the flip side, one person could dive in and start handling everything while the other person twiddles their thumbs on the side. If one person isn't pulling their weight, you're going to see a lot of resentment later.

Set expectations about the relationship just as you would in a marriage. How will you resolve disputes? You're going to fight—don't think you will be the exception. It's absolutely going to happen. You are going to have knock-down, drag-out fights with each other. I have even seen clients almost come to physical blows.

In a marriage, you see your spouse at their absolute best and absolute worst and love them anyway. It's the same in a business relationship. You will see how your business partner deals with the most intense stress, and you should want to work with them anyway.

So how are you going to deal with conflicts? What is that going to look like? Let's visualize.

A TALE OF TWO BUSINESSES

We'll look at two separate client partnerships I've worked with. One is an example of a successful, thriving partnership; the other one was a failure.

THE POST EAST

Tonya originally intended to start her coffee shop with two friends, but when they dropped out, her fiancé Chris stepped in to be her business partner. These brave souls took on business and marriage all in one swoop: They got married just months after opening the shop! They quickly realized working and living together was going to be their greatest challenge.

"I think it forced a lot of issues to the surface," says Tonya. "That stuff you could normally just pretend wasn't there? Stuff like my inability to listen, being too demanding, or being self-centered and egotistical? Those kinds of things will come up because someone else is now engaged in the process and they're calling you on it."

Over time, they established a working relationship and found their most natural roles in the company. Tonya is the face of the business and handles the day-to-day operations, while Chris conducts all the technical and mechanical work. The Post East has been thriving for over three years and specializes in gluten-free, vegan, and organic smoothies and baked goods. About a year ago, Tonya and Chris reached a huge milestone: They were able to purchase the building that houses their business, and now they serve as landlord to the other businesses in the building.

Tonya and Chris already knew each other exceptionally well, and their strong bond led to them becoming strong partners not just in life, but in business.

WAREHOUSE PERSONNEL

In the second example, Kevin and his partner—a longtime friend—decided to go into business together. They wanted to create a warehouse staffing company that would help companies like Amazon find workers for their distribution centers. The company would do the legwork and take care of things such as background checks and employee management.

When the partners came to me, I ran them through my checklist. How long have you known each other? Why are you going into business together? So on and so forth. They passed all my tests. Kevin had the money, and his partner had the know-how and business contacts to get them started. I helped them get everything set up.

Six months later, they were in my office telling me they needed to get divorced. They had irreconcilable differences. It turns out Kevin's partner didn't have the industry knowledge or connections he had promised. Instead, he was expecting his wife to funnel him leads through her job at another staffing agency. When that dried up, he insisted they hire a salesperson to bring in new accounts. This key information was not disclosed to Kevin up front.

Kevin remembers: "He was sitting in his back office doing nothing while the salesperson was out there. He wouldn't answer the phones, send emails, any of that stuff. He would send it all to me, and then he would basically stay at home, raise his horses, and never come to work."

This wasn't the setup Kevin had signed on for. Eventually, he told the partner he needed to either put up some more money or get out. The partner left; Kevin stayed. The split was tame and amicable, compared to many others I've seen.

"He was good with it," says Kevin, "He understood he didn't have the money or the will to do it."

Kevin had known his business partner for a couple of years, but his friend was still able to misrepresent himself and his background. He left Kevin high and dry with a business he knew little about. This could have been avoided with more business planning.

LET'S GET PERSONAL

As I mentioned earlier, when my husband and I got married, our rabbi gave us a relationship questionnaire. We were instructed to fill it out separately, then come together and talk about our answers. I loved this idea so much that I developed a similar method of evaluation for prospective business partners.

This is a prerequisite for working with me. The way it works is very similar to what you might experience in marriage counseling. My clients each complete the quiz on their own, then they come back to me, and we have a conversation together.

The following is an abridged version of my signature questionnaire. The questions really dig in to how you deal with certain business and relationship scenarios, and the point is to generate some dialogue to help you better understand yourself and your partner.

PARTNERSHIP PLANNING QUESTIONNAIRE

*The purpose of this questionnaire is to evaluate and understand how you each function in key areas in your personal and professional lives. The results of this questionnaire should be used to discuss your compatibility as business partners. Each partner should complete the questionnaire **on their own.** Answer as genuinely as you can. Circle all that apply. Feel free to add explanations or additional comments as needed.*

1. I see myself as:
   A. Easygoing, calm, and patient.
   B. A little uptight, easily irritated and could use more patience.

2. I see my partner as:
   A. Easygoing, calm and patient.
   B. A little uptight, easily irritated and could use more patience.

3. How do you generally adapt to change?
   A. With resistance
   B. Quite easily

4. How would you measure your success?
   A. My car and/or house
   B. My career and/or income
   C. My spirituality
   D. The happiness of my family
   E. How many kids I have
   F. My happiness/peace of mind
   G. The amount of love in my life

5. When it comes to compromising, I am generally:
   A. Somewhat stubborn.
   B. Quite flexible.
   C. Rational and fair.

6. Would you strive for equality in your business partnership?
   A. Yes, it's important for each of us to feel we are equal in most aspects.
   B. Yes, for the most part, but I know some things just won't be equal.
   C. If we give each other our best and do not expect much in return, that's what counts—not scale.

7. Do you tend to get defensive when someone gives you constructive criticism?
   A. Not really, I handle it quite well for the most part.
   B. No, I appreciate it.
   C. Yes, but I try not to.
   D. Yes, but it's because that person should not be criticizing me.
   E. Yes, but it's because that person lacks tact.
   F. Yes, but it's because that person criticizes me too much.
   G. No one ever criticizes me.

8. Are you more of a risk-taker, or do you tend to play it safe?
   A. Risk-taker
   B. Play it safe

9. When I realize that I am wrong, I:
   A. Can usually admit it easily.
   B. Sometimes get upset.
   C. Tend to try to find excuses or blame someone.

10. How large does a purchase have to be to need both partners' consent?
    A. Any purchase
    B. Over $250
    C. Over $500
    D. Other _____
    E. It depends on what it is.
    F. If my partner thinks we need it, he/she should have the freedom to purchase without my consent or prior knowledge.

GETTING TO KNOW YOU

There are no right or wrong answers here. These questions are designed to help you spell out your own personal beliefs about business. Understanding these traits about yourself and your partner will help you minimize future conflicts—or at least help you deal with them when they come up.

This also isn't meant to be a comprehensive evaluation of your compatibility as business partners—just a starting point. You still have a lot of work to do when it comes to determining whether you and your partner are meant to be.

CHAPTER 2

DATING

———

Panera was crowded for a sunny Saturday afternoon, but Lance managed to snag a semiprivate booth in the back. A week had passed since their first meeting, and Lance was giddy to see Larissa again. He contemplated the menu, unsure if he should order first or wait for her to arrive. Should he pay for her meal? Would that be weird?

He was still debating with himself when Larissa breezed in. It was a warm spring day, and her flowy dress revealed a full arm of colorful tattoos. To Lance, who had been working in the buttoned-up world of finance for far too long, she looked like a breath of fresh air.

They each ordered a soup and salad combo, ultimately

deciding to pay separately, and finally sat down. A sudden wave of nervousness swept across the table. How to begin?

After a long pause, Larissa broke the ice: "So, what's your favorite cocktail?"

Almost immediately, the conversation began to flow. It was as electric and exciting as the night they'd met. Larissa told Lance about her dream of finally owning her own bar. Her voice was full of passion as she spoke of picking the menu of small plates, creating the right ambiance, and developing the cocktails—not to mention finally being her own boss and making decisions for herself.

Lance told Larissa how he'd always wanted to recreate the bar on the show *Cheers*, except more upscale and with fancier drinks. He imagined owning his own place, sitting at the bar and chatting with regulars each night.

Slowly, they got to know each other, sketching out plans for the bar of their dreams. Romantic, elegant—but trendy, too. They even picked out a name: Twist.

When they finally looked up from their notepad, the sky outside had darkened into twilight. "Oh no, my shift starts in 45 minutes," Larissa realized, grabbing her bag.

As they packed up to leave, Lance could barely contain his excitement. He knew they still had a long road ahead of them and a lot to hash out. But he, at least, felt ready to make a commitment.

TUMBLING HEAD OVER HEELS INTO BUSINESS

Those heady early days of business development can feel just like the start of a new romance. In this preliminary stage, you are just trying to figure out who the other person is and what the business is going to be all about. Everybody is putting their best foot forward. Everything seems perfect—especially the idea itself—and you're probably going to make millions of dollars.

At this point, potential partners are just having a conversation. Most business owners start with the creative aspects, and people get really jazzed about ideas. In Lance and Larissa's case, it might be a neat concept for the bar or a snazzy name—whatever is blowing their hair back about the idea. The more people talk, the more excited they get. They're going to create the greatest bar in the history of bars, or the smartest app, or most brilliant business in history.

It's easy to fall down the rabbit hole at this stage and run away with a fun idea while neglecting the fundamentals, which are the core aspects of this relationship you are committing yourself to. You need to have structured conversations about the nature of your partnership, but most are not interested in this at first.

A lot of the business owners I work with jump in without doing any planning. Some come back later to do all the structuring and strategizing they should have done in the first place. Some never do those things and just fall apart or limp along nervously.

IT'S NOT ALL SUNSHINE AND RAINBOWS

There is a reason we date people before committing to spending a lifetime with them. We need to answer the fundamental question: Am I better off with this person as my partner?

You might already be friends with your potential business partner. You could be married to them, or you could have any other type of relationship. But you must still take the time to business date. Get down and dirty to answer the fundamental question: What is it going to be like to be business married to them?

This is the problem my mom ran up against. She and her partner worked well together for years and years until they didn't anymore. Their business marriage ultimately failed due to a serious personality conflict. It's all great until reality sets in and people's true personalities come out. Once the honeymoon is over, you're going to want to know who you are dealing with.

A crucial concern for her was the feeling that she was carrying her partner. She was working herself ragged while he was spending more and more time on the golf course. When she realized this and how long this had been happening, she started to feel resentful. In any relationship, unattended resentment will grow and grow until it destroys everything. It will kill a marriage, and it will kill a business.

It's important for both partners to realize there is a learning curve. You're not going to work perfectly together from the beginning. It's not going to always be sunshine and rainbows; some days it's going to rain and storm. Realizing this gives both partners a chance to grow as people and as a business. Give each other a little bit of grace and a little bit of space to do that.

DELIGHT MINISTRIES

My client Delight Ministries exemplifies the kind of strong partnership that comes from truly knowing your partner.

The names of the two young women who form this non-profit are both MacKenzie—one goes by Kenz, the other by Mac. They met their freshman year of college at Belmont University, where they started a women's campus ministry. It was so successful that they took it wide, and the program is now on eighty campuses across the country. They've had wild success over the past five years.

The MacKenzies are an example of two partners who understand each other's work styles and personalities perfectly. They have complimentary skill sets and strong communication skills that are remarkable given their youth. Kenz is an idea person, a visionary who comes up with the crazy ideas. Mac is very detail oriented and really tries to ground things.

Mac tells me that, after working together awhile, they recognized each other's strengths and weaknesses and how to compensate for them.

"What's so great about our partnership is that we're both equally passionate about it, and we've been able to say, 'Okay, this is what you're good at, and this is what I'm good at. I'm going to let you excel here, and I will excel here.'"

Watching them interact and play off each other is fantastic to experience, and it shows in the success of the nonprofit. It's clear they each understand how the other communicates and, in an almost unspoken way, how the other operates. Best of all, they truly support each other.

"I'm her biggest cheerleader and number one fan," says Kenz about Mac.

EFFECTIVE COMMUNICATION

People love to say, "Communication is king." All right, but what does that mean? The answer varies because there is no single correct style of communication. You should find what specifically works for you and your partner.

It's important to understand and respect how your partner communicates. It's very difficult to force another person to do things the way you would like, so if the way your partner communicates drives you around the bend, then find a way to deal with this because they are unlikely to change. Communication skills are innate. You only have the power to determine how you will handle your partner's communication style. Adapt to work with their style and find a compromise that works for both of you.

When I asked the MacKenzies how they communicate, they told me about their different styles. One likes to sit down and hash things out on the spot; the other likes to think the issue over carefully, then maybe come back to the table and have a conversation. They each understand how the other likes to operate, and they've worked together to establish their own method of conflict resolution.

Overuse of email is a major factor in communication problems. Email is convenient, but you lose a lot of the tone inherent in spoken language. Oftentimes, written messages can give people the wrong impression. I think it's a poor way to have an important conversation. I use emails to follow up or keep a written record of something, but I save important conversations for face-to-face meetings. I think a lot of issues could be resolved if both parties agreed to meet at a mutual time and place and just talk it out.

Some people avoid doing this because they want to avoid confrontation. If you're afraid of conflict, you have to get over that before you start a business because confrontation is the name of the game here. You are going to have clashes—some of them heated. The sooner it happens, the better, and the sooner you'll get the chance to grow and learn from the situation. Letting issues fester or trying to shove them in a box and pretend they aren't there is not a smart way to deal with problems. This leads to passive-aggressive behavior, resentment, and other toxic problems.

PICK A LANE AND STAY IN IT

One of the reasons people enter partnerships is because they don't believe they can do everything themselves. This other person brings either capital or some new skill set to the table that their partner believes can make the business stronger.

If this sounds like you, then flip the mirror back on yourself. You too are being brought into this partnership because of your own unique skills. Everyone should figure out how and what they can contribute before dividing up the work according to each person's strengths.

You can see this division of labor in most marriages. For example, I handle the finances in my marriage, and my husband handles most of our lawn-care work. We share other responsibilities, like caring for our child and house-work. We divide up our duties, so we both know what we're responsible for at any given time.

Likewise, in a business partnership, it's important we take the time to figure out what the most important duties are and who is going to handle them. Get this down in writing in very clear terms to avoid a lot of arguments down the road. Of course, you can tweak and shift things later as needed, but you really want to define your roles based on your personal strengths.

This is when it's handy to have complementary skill sets, as discussed in Chapter 1. One partner may be the visionary, the big-idea person, the person who comes up with the crazy stuff the business should pursue. Partner number two might be more detail-oriented, the person who looks at partner number one's ideas and says, "How can we actually make this happen?" This is a fantastic setup to have.

Here is an exercise you can do to help define the roles of your partnership:

Take a piece of paper and fold it in half. On one side, write, "Stuff I Want to Do/Stuff Only I Can Do" and list the parts of the business that fall under this category. On the other side, write, "Stuff I Don't Want to Do/Stuff I Don't Know How to Do" and make a similar list. Look at the stuff you want and need to do: That's the basis of your job description. Do this separately, then come together and discuss.

It's great if two partners can come together and say, "You're really good with the numbers and running operations, so you do that. I'm really good with creative stuff and marketing so I'm going to do that."

Once you've figured out your roles, stay in your lane. However, you should look over occasionally to see if your partner needs assistance and to make sure you're both driving down the road at an even pace with each other. It can be a big problem if people start straying from their job description and veering into duties that belong to the other partner. Often this happens because of communication problems. One partner isn't happy with the way the other partner is managing things, and instead of communicating this, they take over.

On the flip side, you'll also have a problem if one partner feels like he is dragging the other along. In this case, he must steer out of his lane because his partner isn't doing the things he agreed to do.

Not doing your fair share might stem from a lack of commitment, but it could also be the result of another issue. Life doesn't care if you are starting a business. Health issues and personal problems might arise and can take time away from your work duties. It's easy to get distracted and find yourself unable to commit to your promises.

I don't think falling behind on your responsibilities is inherently going to kill a business, but this needs to be addressed before it becomes an issue. You might not always be 100 percent committed—are both partners okay with that? What happens if one partner needs to take some time to deal with personal issues? Have those conversations up front, because distraction is inevitable.

MONEY MATTERS

I often tell clients that both partners must be on the exact same page about money. This applies both to big issues—like taking on investors and going into debt—and smaller, day-to-day issues. Small disagreements can turn into massive fights when it comes to money.

First off, there is no way for both parties to manage the books. It's not a task both parties can or should do together, so pick one person to handle the accounting. I believe the other person should still check in so they know what is going on. This is not because you should be monitoring your partner—ideally you should trust your partner completely. It's because you should still be aware of what is happening with the business financially.

Pick one person to take the lead. Here's a personal example I share with all my clients: My husband is terrible with money. He really is. I handle all our finances, and I'm good at it. I like overseeing the money because I enjoy having control. We joined our bank accounts very early on. Comingling funds led to some fights, but we worked out those issues and developed a system before we tied the knot.

One thing I love about him is that if he plans to spend more than about one hundred dollars on anything, he will tell me before he does it. We never agreed that one hundred dollars or more triggered a discussion, it just happened naturally. He doesn't have to, but every time he asks, "Hey, I'm going to spend one hundred and fifty dollars on this thing. Is that cool?" I do the same with him. I can't even imagine how many fights that simple sentence has saved us from.

One of the questions on the questionnaire from the last chapter asks, "What amount do you feel is okay for your partner to spend without telling you?" This is important to spell out because people have very different philosophies when it comes to money. Some are frugal; some spend money like water. Make a point to understand your partner's money style and how it compliments your own.

You also need to talk through *where* you will spend your money. You don't necessarily have to always agree, but you must develop the tools for resolving disagreements. If one partner wants to spend money on a big marketing project and the other partner wants to buy inventory, those are two inherently different things. Have a conversation and work out the best course of action together. Taking the decision into your own hands without consulting with your partner is likely to cause problems.

IF YOU FAIL TO PLAN, YOU PLAN TO FAIL

Part of this due-diligence phase is looking ahead together at the future trajectory of your business. Make sure you are on the same page about where you are headed.

This is a book about relationships, not business planning, but there are many great books and resources that will outline the steps for writing a business plan. The idea of sitting down at your computer with an open Word document, trying to write out what you're going to do sounds like torture for a lot of people. There are many new visual models that can help you conceptualize things better.

Here are two business planning tools that I recommend:

SCORE: A huge collection of templates for writing small-business planning documents.

See https://www.score.org/resource/business-planning-financial-statements-template-gallery.

The Idea Frame: An alternative method of conceptualizing your business's profit potential.

See https://www.michaelburcham.com/resources/the-idea-frame.

Focus on the goals for your business. For nearly everyone, the ultimate goal of a business is to make money. Or, put another way, where do you see yourself personally in a couple of years? Do you have a family? Are you traveling? Are you saving for retirement? Your business will need to make a certain amount of money to help you achieve these personal goals. You are making money so you can live a certain lifestyle, so your business goals need to be in line with your personal goals.

Don't overplan, however. If you try to write out every single detail, you are going to get bogged down. Life just doesn't work that way. Give yourself some space to grow and change and adapt to different circumstances.

Another important thing you can do to help steer your business in the right direction is to find mentors in your field. Mentors are experts with similar backgrounds who can help you better understand your business and offer advice and guidance based on their own experiences. A good mentor will both champion and challenge you.

There are many ways to find these advisors. SCORE, mentioned above, has a fantastic mentorship program. You may come across a mentor through your own networking, or you could hire a professional business coach. A good general resource is your local small business association or the Federal Small Business Administration's website (SBA.gov).

IS THIS BUSINESS EVEN VIABLE?

Remember "Warehouse Personnel"—the partnership that ultimately failed back in Chapter 1? Well, it turns out Kevin's problems didn't end when he booted his business partner.

After the partnership ended, Kevin decided to continue with the business. A year and a half later, I got a call from him. Things weren't going well, and he needed to sell or dissolve the company.

What happened? Kevin had inherited a business he had no background in. His partner had assured him he had the know-how to make it in the industry, but this was a ruse. He hadn't done the business planning needed to make sure the business was viable. They thought they had a good idea, but they didn't do any research to make sure there was a market for their service. When reality set in, Kevin found himself in an unsustainable situation.

"I was a little fish in a big ocean," he said. "There was a lot of competition. They would undercut me because they were big companies, and I didn't have the knowledge."

Eventually, juggling fifty employees and HR and trying to find new sales leads got to be too much. When it became clear the business was never going to be highly profitable, he decided to cut his losses.

Now, it's not my place as a lawyer to evaluate whether a concept is going to be successful or not. This isn't *Shark Tank*, and I'm not Mark Cuban. I will, however, tell you that no matter how brilliant your idea, you should slow down and do your homework.

It's not necessary to sit down and write out a formal business plan per se, but do your research to find out if the business is sustainable, viable, and scalable. Do people *want* the service or product you are offering? Are they going to pay for it?

GETTING TO KNOW THE REAL YOU

A lot of the work in this chapter centers on knowing how you and your partner work as a unit. But before you can do that, you need to know yourself. I recommend both partners take the following two well-known assessments, then discuss their results together. These assessments will shine a spotlight on both your strengths and weaknesses. The point of this exercise is to prepare you for what's going to come and to help bridge the communication gap. This isn't a substitute for spending time with someone, but it is a good jumping-off point.

The first is the Myers-Briggs® personality assessment. It uses Jungian psychology to categorize people in one of sixteen distinct personality types. Your personality type is representative of both the way you see the world and your communication style.

The second is the DiSC® assessment, which many companies use to screen potential employees. While Myers-Briggs is a personality test, DiSC® assesses behavior. It's a tool to get to know yourself and your reactions in interpersonal situations. There are fifteen behavioral patterns with names like "counselor," "promoter," and "perfectionist."

Again, the goal is to understand your strengths and weaknesses at a fundamental level. These tests will not only help you better understand yourself and your partner, but they can help you understand the business roles you are best suited for.

Don't be afraid to think outside of your past experiences when determining what roles you are best suited for. If you've never done something before, how do you know if you are any good at it? My mother, for example, said she wasn't very good at business development, which is odd because she is extremely extroverted and personable. She got better in this role over time when she realized she needed to. It may take time to find your ideal role, and these tests can help point you in the right direction.

FROM ENTREPRENEUR TO CEO

When I started my practice, I was the lead and only attorney, so I was doing all the work myself. I was the head of marketing. I was the CFO. I was the CEO. I was the HR Department. I did every single thing for my business.

Once you start growing, however, you simply cannot do everything yourself. You should start outsourcing or delegating certain tasks. This is necessary in any business that is going to survive and prosper.

Some people are not well suited for the transition from doing everything in the business to working on behalf of the business, which is what distinguishes an entrepreneur from a CEO.

The person who is rolling up her sleeves and doing the day-to-day work is the entrepreneur. Your CEO is future-facing and is working to expand the business and bring in new opportunities. The person who starts the business may not end up being its CEO, and that can be very difficult for some owners to accept.

The goal is to create a profitable and successful business. You don't want to stand in the way of that by putting yourself in the wrong position. Use your personal strengths to help the business thrive.

DO YOU EVEN NEED A BUSINESS PARTNER?

Recently, I asked my mom why she'd taken on a business partner in the first place.

"Because I had never started a business before," she said. "It was a crutch. If you have somebody else to go in with you, it spreads the risk. But I would never partner again. Now I know I don't need anybody else."

My mom's point is this: At the end of the day, you can do anything you want to do in business by yourself if you have the self-confidence and determination.

I'm not telling you this to scare you off. After all, the purpose of dating is to figure out who you are. At the same time, it's essential to figure out who you are *together* and how that will influence the business.

Ask yourself: Do I really need this person?

When it comes to choosing a partner, know yourself and take the right steps. Know where your inadequacies lie and what role your counterpart should fill to make a complete package.

Take your time with the dating process and get a clear picture of your needs, who you are partnering with, and how the partnership will further your success.

CHAPTER 3

PROPOSAL AND PRENUP

It was a lovely evening for a hockey game. The air was crisp, the stars were out, and a win was predicted for the Nashville Predators.

Hockey wasn't really Larissa's thing, but she'd let Lance drag her along anyway. He seemed excited, and she didn't want to rain on his parade.

Lance and Larissa had spent weeks feeling each other out and were cautiously edging toward commitment. They'd met with mentors, filled out questionnaires, and taken personality tests. They'd talked through every step at length. Now they were just biding their time, getting to know each other a bit better, and trying to see if they were a good fit. They were having fun.

Larissa held their craft beers while Lance bought them popcorn. They cheered for the Preds and goofed around as the periods dragged on.

During the break before fourth period, Larissa grabbed her bag and said, "I'll go get us some hotdogs."

"Wait!" Lance yelped, grabbing her arm and gesturing towards the ice. "Look over there!"

Up on the Jumbotron, large letters blinked: HAPPY BIRTHDAY, SKYLAR! Larissa looked at Lance quizzically.

"No, look now."

LARISSA, WILL YOU BE MY BUSINESS PARTNER?

"Oh my god, you're so corny, Lance," Larissa said, a giant smile spreading across her face. "Yes! Yes, of course I will!"

They jubilantly shook hands. "You've just made me the happiest businessman in the world," Lance beamed.

"Well, enjoy the moment," Larissa replied. "Starting tomorrow, we have a lot of work to do."

MAKING IT OFFICIAL

Deciding to go into business together might seem like the culmination of all your hard work, but it's really just the beginning. When Lance, Larissa, or any other excited set of partners turn to me to make things official, we have a lot of steps to go through to get their business off on the right foot.

Now is the time to bring in the professionals. At this point in the process, you definitely need to visit a lawyer to help set up a formal agreement. We will set you up with the corporate entity and contracts you need. This is one of the most important things you should do for your business and your partnership. If you go into business without any sort of formal agreement, you are asking for a world of hurt later.

THE SCALE OF LIABILITY

The first thing we must do is choose a corporate entity. I generally recommend that most of my clients think about incorporating right away. Here is why:

Do you remember after 9/11 when the Department of Homeland Security came out with their color-coded terror threat advisory system—or as I like to call it, the "terror scale"? The point of the terror scale is that different colors signify different levels of threat. Red is really bad, blue is not so bad, but it's all still terror.

I have a similar scale that I call my Scale of Liability. Every single business that exists has liability, and some have more than others. For example, businesses involving food are high liability businesses. Any time a human being is going to consume something, a myriad of things could go wrong. Anything hospitality-related is on the higher side of the liability scale, red or orange.

On the blue-green side of the scale, you might have a professional blogger. There are still potential issues: defamation, intellectual property infringement, etc. But the chances of something happening and it being detrimental to your business and to you personally are not as pervasive.

But again, it's all terror. Everyone has liability.

Lance and Larissa are particularly at risk. Not only will they be serving food, they have alcoholic beverage liability. Most jurisdictions have a Dram Shop Act, which means that if someone gets really drunk at your bar, drives, and kills somebody, the family can sue the bar for letting them drink too much.

Having a corporate entity provides what I like to call a

Great Wall of China protecting you and your personal assets. If someone decides to sue your business for some reason, they will bring the lawsuit against the business itself and not you personally. Your house, car, family, and investments will be shielded.

An LLC won't shield you from everything. For example: I have an LLC for my law firm. However, if someone is going to sue me for malpractice, my LLC can't protect me from that. It can protect me if someone walks into my office, slips, and falls because they would sue the business—not me personally.

So, we need to protect our baby business from the many terrors of liability. We do that by forming a corporate entity.

THE MANY FLAVORS OF CORPORATE ENTITIES

The question is: What are the different kinds of business setups, and how do I pick one? What are the options?

A couple things to note before we dive in: Every state offers different flavors of corporate formation. The options and how you apply can vary from state to state, so this is just a general overview. If you Google "Secretary of State" and your home state, you can find out how to get started where you are.

Here are your basic options:

UNINCORPORATED PARTNERSHIPS

The section above lays out a pretty convincing argument about why I recommend everyone incorporate. But what if, against my best advice, you decide not to?

If you do not incorporate, then the law would consider you and your partner to have a general partnership—or a sole proprietorship if you were going into business alone. There are many different variations of this, depending on the partnership agreement you sign, but in general there are two different types:

A general partnership means both parties are equal. They share liability risk equally. Under most state laws regarding partnerships, unless there is an agreement in place between the partners (a partnership contract), the partners share both the profits and the losses 50/50. I have had many partners come in to see me and tell me all about how they split everything 70/30 or 60/40 or whatever and then come to find out this is a verbal agreement—not one in writing. I like to say their verbal agreement is worth just as much as the paper it is written on. (Chuckle, lawyer joke!)

A limited partnership is one where one person is providing the money (the limited partner) and the other person is doing the business management (the general partner). If there is a lawsuit in this scenario, the limited partner is only liable up to the amount of money they've put into the business. The general partner is liable for pretty much everything else since they are the one running the business.

BENEFIT CORPORATION (B-CORP)

A benefit corporation isn't recognized in every jurisdiction, but it is becoming more popular.

It is a for-profit company that also has some sort of social benefit. Warby Parker is an example of a benefit corporation: For every pair of glasses they sell, they give a pair of glasses to someone in a developing country. The distinguishing feature of the B-Corp is that the business must consider both profit and social consequences when making decisions.

Forming a B-Corp is mostly a good PR move, but there are certain reporting requirements depending on your jurisdiction. If your business has some sort of social mission, you may want to consider this kind of corporation.

The majority of businesses, however, will go with one of the following options:

CORPORATION (C-CORP AND S-CORP)

Corporations come in two subflavors. The main difference comes down to taxes.

A traditional corporation is a C-Corp. If you form your corporation and don't do anything else, you are going to be subject to double taxation: The money your business makes will be taxed at a corporate level, and then when the shareholders pull out money, it will be taxed a second time.

I find that for most small businesses C-Corps are not ideal. They are better for larger, more complex organizations.

Both the S-Corp and the LLC discussed below are pass-through tax entities, meaning you are not taxed at the corporate level. The money passes directly to you and is taxed at your personal rate. This makes these organizations better suited for small businesses.

S-Corps consider the people running the business (you and your partner in this case), to be employees of the business. You would get W-2s and would be subject to withholding. This makes life much easier come tax time.

If you are going to employ other people at your business right away, then I sometimes recommend an S-Corp.

S-Corps have more reporting requirements than an LLC. Some states require you to keep meeting minutes and to set up payroll right away and take payroll taxes out. If you don't have an accounting background, this could get complicated quickly. Many companies that are just starting out aren't necessarily paying themselves a regular salary, which can also complicate payroll setup.

LIMITED LIABILITY CORPORATION (LLC)

LLCs are a bit of a misnomer. Although they are called limited liability corporations, you are most often just as protected with an LLC as you are with a regular corporation.

For small business owners, an LLC is the best of both worlds. It's as easy to create and run as a sole proprietorship, but you get all the protections of a corporation. They are very easy to set up in most states—just fill out the Articles of Organization and pay a fee. Probably 90 percent of the corporate setup I do is LLC related.

With an LLC, you as the principal have to pay estimated self-employment taxes to the IRS every quarter.

YOU NEED AN ACCOUNTANT

You need an accountant right away. You really, really,

really do. My mother always told me, "You can't do anything in business without your lawyer and accountant in the same room." This is very true, and I advise all my clients to get an accountant right away because this stuff can get really complicated—fast.

If you're waffling between an LLC and an S-Corp, the tiebreaker is going to be your accountant. Go find one, ask them this very straightforward question, and then get started on setting up your books. It's kind of like getting a joint-account before you get married.

In Lance and Larissa's situation, I think we are probably looking at an S-Corp. They will be paying employees right out of the gate, and Lance has a financial background that would enable him to handle all the regulations and corporate formalities. If, however, he did not have that background, I might recommend an LLC.

THE PRENUPTIAL AGREEMENT

Now we move on to the contract between you and your partner. This is very important to get right.

Once we form this partnership, you are essentially married. This contract is something you absolutely need to go to an attorney to sort out. Don't just pull a contract off the Internet and call it done. Get someone who can really talk you through the details.

A lot of people have the money conversation first because money is always front and center in people's minds. But that is just the start. In a prenuptial agreement we're talking about a lot of really important things: What assets are each of you bringing to the marriage? How are you going to split things up if things go south? Who will take care of the business child? Will there be alimony payments?

You will want to review your partnership agreement on a yearly basis, just as you might reevaluate your insurance policy (or at least you should be evaluating your insurance policy every year!). As things grow and change, the original agreement may not fit with your current situation. Your agreement can absolutely be modified and amended. You can even rewrite the whole thing if you want to. At the end of every year, pull it out and see if anything needs to be amended, changed, or taken out.

A QUICK TERMINOLOGY NOTE

From a legal stand point, if we're talking about partners who have not formed any corporation, they are called partners and have a partnership agreement. If we have a corporation, a B-Corp, S-Corp, or C-Corp, then the people who run it are called shareholders. Finally, if we're talking about an LLC, the people who run it are generally called members, possible managers, or directors. Their agreement is called an operating agreement.

That said, for the purposes of this book, we're just going to use the terms "partner" and "partnership agreement" whether we are referencing an incorporated or unincorporated entity. The stuff that goes into it, whichever flavor you choose, is pretty much the same.

HOW MUCH ARE WE GETTING PAID?

Everyone's favorite subject. Obviously how much everyone is getting paid will be in there. We need to figure out how much everyone is going to be paid and what percentage of equity everyone receives.

There are a couple of different ways to figure out who is going to get paid what. A lot of times for small businesses, neither partner takes any salary until the business starts to make a profit. After that, we can amend the contract.

As the business becomes more stable after the initial startup phase, I encourage everybody to set a minimum guaranteed payment on a monthly basis or quarterly basis so that there is a benchmark. The minimum may change over time.

WHO IS IN CHARGE?

Then, there's the equity split. Put simply: What percentage of the company does each of you own?

This really comes down to decision-making and what happens if you decide to sell the business. From a decision-making perspective, it's important to understand that if somebody owns 90 percent of the business, their majority ownership means that they can make decisions even against the wishes of the minority partner.

So how can we split the equity between partners?

NOT 50/50

Most businesses have a majority and minority owner. Usually the person who puts in more money would get the majority stake in the company.

The majority owner has a lot of power—but as a minority owner, you still have rights. The majority owner has to respect that and not abuse his power. Overarching all of this are fiduciary duties of good faith and loyalty towards the business. You can't do things to purposely hurt the business.

I really believe there is no such thing as a true 50/50 partnership. It's very rare. We can do 50/50 on paper, but oftentimes that's not what the business looks like, practically speaking. Usually one person is ponying up the money, and one person is putting in the sweat, meaning they are coming to the table with some sort of skill or expertise.

Sweat equity just isn't equivalent to money capital. Someone can work themselves completely insane, but it takes cold hard cash to start a business, so the person bringing the financial contribution usually ends up getting more equity in the business. This makes sense because they are investing a good portion of their personal funds and need to make that back in some shape or form, either as a chunk of the profits, or with larger equity when the business ultimately sells.

However, this split might change over time. Someone may invest $50,000 in a business, but five years later, they may have done nothing but put in the money while the other partner has put in years of hard work.

50/50

If we decide to go with a 50/50 split, things can get more complicated. Basically, if you're 50/50 and one partner is digging in their heels about a decision and it can't be resolved, we have a deadlock. If I have clients who really want to be 50/50, I have them make a list of all the decisions that need to be unanimous. Some of those decisions include taking on another partner, buying real estate, incurring any sort or expense over a specific dollar amount, dissolving the business, or going into debt. Basically, any really big decision needs to be considered.

In another section, we might spell out, "These decisions belong to partner A, and these to partner B." That way, the partners don't need to consult each other to make those decisions.

HOW WILL WE HANDLE CONFLICTS?

A good partnership agreement will help guide partners through disagreements within the company. It's very important we don't back ourselves into a corner where the business can't move forward because of a deadlock. If parents had a baby and they couldn't agree on what to feed it, then it would starve to death. We must do what's necessary to save the business.

Most partnership agreements I write say that if partners are in a deadlock situation and it persists for a certain amount of time, then a series of events will be triggered. These events are designed to help you break the deadlock or dissolve the business if it can't be resolved.

HOW DO WE SPLIT UP?

Just like in a real prenup, this is an important thing to consider: What do we do if the worst happens? Basically, who is getting full custody of the kid?

Unfortunately, I rarely see partnerships end super amicably.

People's priorities change over time. If at any point one partner wants out and one partner wants to maintain the business, we're entering buy-sell territory.

In this situation, what can cause a lot of conflicts is that one partner is unhappy and wants out, and the other partner wants to keep the business. If one partner wants to keep running the business and the other one intends to leave, the remaining partner is going to have to pay the exiting partner for their interests.

People ask, "Can't I just kick my partner out?" No, you can't just do that. There are ways to expel partners from partnerships, but you must tread very carefully. If they are taking actions detrimental to the business, you might be able to remove them from their decision-making capabilities. But here's the rub that drives people crazy: Even if you're able to remove them, you can't take away their financial interests. This is hard for people to understand, but when you are a member of an LLC or a shareholder, you own a piece of property. You can't hold or touch it, but it's a piece of property and is worth something.

To fully untangle yourself from someone, you will probably have to pay them for their property. The same thing happens when you get divorced from your spouse: You have to pay them.

You're also probably going to want a noncompete and nonsolicitation clause to make sure they don't go around the corner and start a competing business with the knowledge they've picked up over the years or try to take your customers or employees with them when they leave.

What if you are the one who wants to leave? Often in my partnership agreements, I will put a right-of-first refusal clause. This means that the exiting partner must offer their interest in the company to the other partner first. If that person declines, then they can try to sell it on the open market. Even then, the remaining partner has the right to accept or deny the new person, because they get to have a say in who they do business with.

What happens if we want to split and nobody wants the business? Then we would want to dissolve it. There is a very specific way that must be done, and it's laid out in the partnership agreement. We will talk more about this in Chapter 8.

There are other reasons you might need to dissolve a business or replace a partner, such as the death of a partner or a retirement. Oftentimes, I build triggering events into the contract. A death of one of the partners would trigger a succession of things to happen. The operating agreement guides us through all these motions.

WHO OWNS WHAT? (MARITAL PROPERTY)

For some reason, almost every partnership dissolution I've dealt with has involved a conflict over something physical. Let's call it a widget, because it's usually some inconsequential thing. My client wants it back. It's an obsession. They will die on the hill just to get the damn thing back.

Just like in a marriage, certain assets you bring into the business can be considered marital property. Say one partner brings in a bunch of computers. It can become murky whether they belong to him or the business later on.

If you buy large pieces of equipment, it needs to be in the partnership agreement that you paid for it with your own funds and that you want it back if something happens.

WHEN CONTRACTS GO RIGHT

Molly and Lyndi met at a food entrepreneurship class. Lyndi was originally planning to open a bakery and bar, while Molly was workshopping a healthy meal preparation business. They found themselves drawn to one another and eventually decided to open an event catering company together called Juniper Green.

These two ladies were really model clients when it came to forming a business partnership. They did their due diligence, had deep, meaningful conversations about my partnership questionnaire, and even went on a business date test dinner together.

When they decided to finally tie the knot and get business married, we sat down and worked on their operating agreement. These two then did something I just love: They each went back to their own corners and had their own lawyers take a look at the contract, which is a great idea if you can afford it. I represent the business, but it's always a good idea to have someone else looking out for your personal interests.

They came back to me with a few revisions and questions. I love when that happens because it means that the client has read the contract thoroughly. Some people don't even read their contracts and just sign them. This is a terrible idea.

Molly said the process of creating their partnership agreement actually brought them closer: "I think it created some opportunities for trust building. Because we both had to look at our own lives and situations and say, 'Okay, what's the worst scenario for me personally?'"

Juniper Green is still a very new business, but I'm optimistic about its future. Molly and Lyndi's business acumen, willingness to do the legwork, and strong bond bode well for what lies ahead.

THANK ME LATER

This stuff is difficult to think about, but it is so important.

When you're in the throes of early business love, you don't want to think about these difficult questions, but it is so important. Nobody wants to have a conversation about what happens if their new business fails. It's similar to how everyone knows they need a will but nobody wants to have a conversation about their own death.

You could date for years, finally get married, and then realize, "God, this is not the person I want to spend my life with." Even the most careful among us can end up in that situation. We sign an agreement so we can very clearly outline what to do in these situations.

But you need to have these hard conversations at the beginning and play all those scenarios out. As painful as it is, I guarantee that working it out on paper is so much less painful than experiencing it. Doing the work now might save you from going through that nightmare later.

CHAPTER 4

MARRIED BLISS

——

The big night had finally arrived. Lance felt like he had been waiting for this moment his whole life.

Twist was finally open. The space was strung with twinkling lights, and colorful cocktails dotted the tables. The bar was polished, gleaming, and full of potential. All around him, Nashville's hottest tastemakers, bloggers, and Instagram stars buzzed.

He leaned against the bar, a rosemary gin fizz in his hand. His eye caught Larissa's across the room. She was expertly wielding a cocktail shaker, whipping up a custom drink while chatting with new patrons.

She smiled at him and mouthed, "We did it!"

Maybe it was the three cocktails he'd already sampled, but he felt his heart swell. It hadn't been easy. They'd visited dozens of spaces before settling on this one. There had been long weeks meeting with interior decorators, choosing menus, and hiring staff. Luckily, Larissa truly knew what she was doing. With his funds and her know-how, things had come together beautifully.

Now people were shaking his hand, congratulating him on his new business venture. People were promising to come by every weekend, and there was talk of a write-up in *Nashville Living*. He couldn't wait to get deep into the day-to-day business of owning a bar.

He'd never been so happy.

THE STRESS OF NEW BEGINNINGS

Launching a new business can be a mixed bag of emotions.

On the one hand, it's thrilling. It's the culmination of all your work so far. You feel ecstatic. You're in business love with your new partner, and everything is just going awesome.

At the same time, the first six months of running a business can be incredibly stressful. There is so much you must learn and quickly adapt to, I often liken it to drinking out of a firehose. Every single day is the most exciting and terrifying day of your life. That can be tough to deal with as an individual, but now you are also in the trenches alongside someone else.

In the case of Lance and Larissa, they are busy serving customers, trying to make sure their systems are working, doing payroll, doing marketing, just doing everything. They are wearing seventeen different hats, and everything is new each day.

It's no surprise that this is also when Lance and Larissa might experience their first big disagreement. Everything was sunshine and rainbows when they were picking out paint swatches and cocktail glasses, but now they are deep into the day-to-day decision-making. If they are lucky, they will remember the conversations I asked them to have in the earlier chapters, and when a disagreement does come up, they have the tools to resolve it.

You need to choose your battles. I like to tell my clients not to get stuck debating over every small decision. It's easy to get bogged down at this stage, but if there's no risk of death or severe bodily harm, then it's time to make a call and move on.

Now, more than ever, it's important to do the work to maintain your relationship even as you build your business.

KEEPING THE SPARK ALIVE

This is a pivotal time to make sure you're putting good relationship habits in place. You're not just growing a business here—you're building a marriage, too. You want to get your working relationship off on the right foot.

To go back to my analogy of your business as a baby, launching your business is a lot like bringing the new baby home from the hospital. Suddenly everything is about the baby, everyone wants to see the baby, and you're busy caring for the baby. It's very easy to neglect your relationship with your partner as you pour all your energy into childcare.

However, it's more important than ever to care for your partner now, too. You need to constantly check in with your relationship to make sure things are still working and to keep the lines of communication open.

Now is a good time to check in with your business mentors for a little couples therapy. Schedule meetings with your mentor together so you can all work through any issues that come up in these early days.

Previously unexplored facets of your relationship might become more apparent now as you go through the motions of running a business on a daily basis. You may have gotten in the habit of being around each other twenty-four hours a day and then discover you now need some space. Some people just need alone time, and that's not personal. It's important to respect the needs of your partner and to honor your own feelings, too.

Let's talk about a couple of my most successful client relationships and what they attribute their success to.

SHARED GOALS, DELEGATED RESPONSIBILITIES

Let me start by introducing you to some of my favorite clients, and the nicest people you will ever meet. If this book had a poster child, it would be the family behind 312 Pizza Company.

Staci and Dan Bockman were Chicago transplants who were always searching for real deep-dish pizza in Nashville. Finding nothing, they decided to create their own recipes for family and friends. Their pizza was so great, they decided to take it to the masses.

They started a family-owned business with *five* partners: Staci and Dan, Staci's mother and father, and her sister.

So, we have multiple partners, and they are all family. This could be a recipe for disaster, but they make it look easy.

First, they opened 312 Pizza Company in Germantown. A year or two later, they opened a chocolate shop, called Tempered Café and Chocolate. They make truffles, chocolates, and this aerated sponge candy I like to call "crack." I have told them they can pay their legal fees in this stuff—it is that amazing! Tempered is Stacy's baby, and she spends most of her time there. On weekend evenings, the chocolate shop turns into an absinthe bar called The Green Hour. It's very cool.

Now they are busy opening a second location for 312, as well as a breakfast restaurant called Maple and Eggs. To say they have been successful is an understatement, but it's not always smooth sailing.

Staci tells me, "Honestly there are some moments when we're sitting around the kitchen table, menu planning, and papers fly, tempers fly. Yes, we've had some fights, because we're all very passionate about what we believe the restaurants should be."

Part of the reason they have held everything together is because they have carefully defined everyone's role in the company. Staci tells me everyone had to pick their lane and stay in it.

"We decided right from the beginning we were going to pick one person to be the general manager, and the general manager is the one who oversees everything in the restaurant."

Her husband Dan fills that role while she does sales and marketing. Her sister coordinates events, her mother does payroll and admin, and her father used to do the maintenance and physical work.

They've had their share of challenges, too. They lost Stacy's father after a long battle with esophageal cancer. He left a gaping emotional and physical hole in the company and family. But they rallied together, and Dan took over many of his responsibilities.

Recently, Dan was diagnosed with cancer and must fly out of state for treatment on a weekly basis. As a result, the company had to delegate some of the day-to-day responsibilities so they could focus on being healthy and growing their business. They did this by hiring a general manager to take care of day-to-day operations, allowing them to focus on taking care of themselves and their company.

I am happy to say that Dan's tumor has shrunk enough to be operable, and we are all very optimistic he is going to be cancer free within a few months.

CLOSER THAN FAMILY

What I found interesting with 312 is they don't have in-fighting among the family, or at least they aren't coming to me with petty nonsense.

One thing I've discovered over time is that family businesses generally do better in the long run. It doesn't matter if it's husbands and wives, brothers, or extended family—my family-run businesses rarely come to me with any issues.

At first, I thought that was odd. I would never go into business with my husband because we would kill each other in five seconds. But I figured it out once I was married: Families are used to fighting with each other. They know a small disagreement is not going to totally derail things, so they deal with it and move on. This is in stark opposition to some of my nonmarried partners who are willing to die on each and every hill. The challenge with family businesses is creating a work-life balance.

Staci explains, "I can see that because you are always

talking about work. Then you'll end up in this bad mood because something bad happened at work and you want to keep talking about it at home. Whereas when you have separate jobs and then when you come home, you can leave your stuff at work more easily. In our situation, stuff comes home because these businesses are our lives."

Staci says it's all about your dynamic as a family before you go into business.

"If you have that kind of family where you already have a great relationship, adding a work element to it is not hard, as long as you define the roles. I can say if you are already a family that's always butting heads, don't do it. There's just no reason to do it. If you can't work through family stuff, how are you going to work through business stuff?"

DEEPER RELATIONSHIPS THROUGH BUSINESS

I think friends probably have the highest rate of failure in business partnerships. It's tough because you have a personal relationship that means something, but it's not as intimate as a marriage or a family bond. There is a lot of potential for things to get ugly if you aren't careful.

On the other hand, you have some partners like the MacKenzies from Delight Ministries who have really used their business as an opportunity to grow and mature together. They are a great example of two business partners whose relationship has deepened over time. They have always been good friends, but their bond has matured thanks to a shared commitment and a deep understanding of each other.

The two girls met back in college, which means they have gone through some pivotal life stages together. Running a business with someone else is hard. It's even harder when you're navigating through your early twenties.

Mac and Kenz were roommates when they first started Delight. After their business became a full-time job, they found they needed to pull away a bit and put some boundaries between their work and personal life. They still hang out as friends, but they've started to separate their social circles a bit more and give each other space, especially after spending long weeks on the road traveling for work. They also make time to keep the "romance" alive in their relationship.

"Sometimes, we've found we have to take a weekend or a week and have fun together and not do work," says Mac.

Which is not to say they don't have disagreements. With a growing company, there are a lot of decisions to be made and a lot of unknowns, which can lead to frustration. They handle their conflicts by remembering their divergent communication styles. While Kenz likes to confront issues head on, Mac likes to take some time and space to work out solutions privately. At the same time, they aren't afraid to get to the root of a problem, whether it's business or personal.

"Sometimes, it's putting aside the work stuff for a second and asking, 'Okay, what's really going on here?' I think that has really helped us so many times. Because we're such good friends, we know each other on such a personal level to know that there's probably something else going on there," says Mac.

In the end, what keeps them together is their love for their job.

"I think partnership comes down to equal passion in what you're doing. You have to believe the vision," says Mac. "At the end of the day, I know she's just as passionate about Delight as I am. No matter what issues we face, that shared passion brings us back into equilibrium."

CHECKING IN

I am a firm believer that any business meetings should

have an agenda as well as a firm start and end time. If they don't, how will you know you have accomplished anything? The same is true of checking in with your partner.

First, I would set a recurring weekly calendar event either at the start or end of the week, depending on your business. This way, you won't be tempted to do something else during that time. (Sidebar: This process also works REALLY well if you are trying to schedule time for the gym!) The following is a sample agenda of what I would recommend partners discuss during these weekly meetings:

1. Check in With Each Other
    A. Each person shares one thing from their personal lives.
    B. Each person shares one success from the week or one thing they wish to accomplish in the week ahead.
    C. Each person shares one frustration from the week or one thing they think is going to be frustrating in the coming week.

2. Financial Check-In
    A. Review:
        i.   Profit and Loss statement
        ii. Balance sheet
        iii. Cash Flow
            a. Make sure you both know what these are and how to review them properly.
            b. Have your accountant on the phone for the first few meetings to walk you through.
        iv. Review your key performance indicators and how you are doing in each category.
            a. If any one category is identified as an issue, come up with an action plan to address it.

3. People
    A. If you have employees, review employee performance for the week, identify any issues, and map out how they will be addressed.
    B. Review customer satisfaction, identify any issues, and map out how they will be addressed.

4. Future
    A. Review three-month, six-month, and one-year goals.
    B. Report on progress on goals.
    C. Identify any areas where you need to pivot to get back on track for goals.

Some of these points you may not need to cover every week, such as the financials. Some may only need to be covered once a month. If you follow a similar schedule each week, it will eventually become routine.

Have one partner take notes during these meetings and provide them to each partner at the conclusion of the meeting. Google Docs is a great way to keep a shareable, running document.

A STRONGER UNION

When your business first launches, you may find yourself dealing with a whirlwind of emotions. It's a happy and stressful time, and you may also be going through some individual reflection and discovery during this period. You may learn things about yourself that you didn't realize.

I often tell my clients there is a pretty good chance their business isn't going to look or feel exactly like they imagined it. That's not a bad thing. The important thing is to keep moving forward.

This is a make-or-break time for a lot of business relationships. But at the same time, it's a golden opportunity to strengthen your bond while you work together to achieve your shared goals.

CHAPTER 5

HONEYMOON'S OVER

———

The Friday evening shift always seemed to drag on endlessly. The buzzing happy-hour crowd was quickly followed by the date-night couples, then the last-call crowd. It was exhausting.

Tonight was particularly bad. A server called in sick, so it was all hands on deck. The bar was packed, and Larissa almost tripped twice as she made her way through the crowd taking drink orders and delivering plates of olives and cheese. She'd been working all day, and her feet were on fire.

Lance was nowhere in sight.

This wasn't surprising. Lance had become a rarer and rarer sight around Twist lately. In contrast, Larissa felt like she lived there. She was the first one there every morning and stayed past closing each evening. She'd barely seen her dog all month, and she kept forgetting to eat.

Yesterday, Lance rolled in around 1:00 PM, obviously hungover. He seemed to be treating the bar like his own personal watering hole, holding court and handing out free drinks to his favorite regulars. It was always a party when Lance was around, but Larissa worried that Twist was the one picking up the tab.

Larissa wouldn't even mind that much—she had signed on to run the day-to-day operations after all—but other things were slipping, too. Lance had agreed to take care of all the financials, but several employees were complaining about late paychecks. A quick peek at the books showed a disorganized mess. She'd been straightening everything out during what should have been her afternoon break.

Larissa knew she should say something to Lance, but she didn't really want to rock the boat. After all, things had been going so well up until a few weeks ago. Maybe they could get back to the way things used to be.

Until then, she had tables to bus.

A MATTER OF TRUST

Why is it so easy for a good relationship to turn sour?

Usually when a business relationship fails, it's due to a combination of factors: a rough patch in the business, someone not pulling their weight, or a fundamental failure in communication. Most of these reasons can be boiled down to a lack of respect or trust between the partners.

Even if you've known this person your entire life, even if they are a friend or family member, I look at entering into a business relationship as if it's a brand-new relationship. You still need to go through the steps to establish trust on both sides.

Let's talk about some of the ways business relationships fail and how we can get them back on track.

COMMUNICATION FAILS

Failures in communication are one of the biggest problems I see among my clients. You can trace a lot of issues back to the moment partners stop communicating with each other.

There's a lot of talk going into business. You have weekly meetings at Starbucks or Panera where you sit and plan your business. Then, once things are in motion, the meetings drop off. You're so consumed with doing business, you forget that you need to continue fostering that scheduled communication.

I know there is trouble brewing when I get pulled into conversations. Clients start cc'ing me on their email communications, which is a pretty good indicator they are no longer talking verbally. If you're only communicating via email and text with someone you see literally every day, that is a pretty bad sign that the boat is already taking on water.

Having a set of guidelines for communication is the best way to avoid falling into that trap. It's a good idea to schedule weekly check-ins with each other. This is time spent away from the actual business to discuss how everybody is doing and how they feel about various issues. You can follow my outline in Chapter 4.

Be warned: There is a danger of taking this principle too far and getting bogged down in every little decision. Think back to the 312 clan and their clear delineation of roles and responsibilities. If everyone's role is well defined, you don't have to constantly hash out every disagreement. You can clearly delegate group decisions and individual decisions. The manager can make managerial decisions, and the marketer can make marketing decisions. If there is a decision concerning the overall growth and vision of the company, then that is a discussion for everybody.

Communication can be a moving target, but you need to figure out what works well for you and your partner.

FINANCIAL FAILS

Money is the downfall of so many relationships—both in romance and business.

A lot of financial issues can be headed off early on by making sure you and your partner are on the same page. If one partner is more frugal and one likes to spend money like it's on fire, then you have a fundamental personality issue you need to catch before it metastasizes into huge resentment.

My husband and I combined our finances ten months before we got married. That is a bit unorthodox, but it was one of the best things we ever did because it forced us to stop thinking about our income as *your* money and *my* money and start thinking about it as *our* money. We had to quickly develop a system for managing our spending.

Similarly, every business needs to work out some fundamental money issues: What types of things can Partner A spend money on? What about Partner B? If my husband goes to buy dog food, he doesn't have to clear that with me. But if he wants to drop a large sum of money on one of his hobbies, then yeah, he probably should—and vice versa. It has to be a two-way street.

So, if Lance decides to buy an expensive shuffleboard table without Larissa's consent, that could be a problem. They don't need it, it's big, and maybe they don't have a good place for it. Larissa might be (rightly) upset. I've had situations in which a business is struggling financially, and one of the partners unilaterally decides to go to the bank and get a new line of credit, fills out the paperwork, and just goes to their partner for a signature. That's a financial and communication failure.

"Hey, partner, you went to the bank to talk to someone about our business and financial needs without me?"

Developing a good relationship around money is all about figuring out things like, "How much communication do I need to trust you? How much control can we each have over finances so I can trust you?" A good rule of thumb when you are just starting out is to clear most, if not all, purchases with each other to establish an air of transparency early on. As you get further along and start trusting how you each handle financial decisions, then you can decide what types of things you each need to communicate about and which you can just make a call on individually.

MISALIGNED GOALS

Sometimes, everybody starts out on the same page in terms of goals and visions for the business, and this outlook changes over time. As a small business owner myself, I can tell you that six years in, my business looks totally different than what I imagined it would.

Unfortunately, you can do all the planning in the world, but things change and people's lives change. This can be a difficult thing to grapple with.

One way to try to avoid this is by making sure you know your business partner well from the outset. I have one client who came into my office who is on his third failing partnership. Just like if someone were to have three failed marriages, he needs to ask himself: Where am I going wrong?

Well, I asked him how long he had known each of those partners. He told me six to eight weeks each.

I've been with my husband five years now. I feel like I

know him as well as anyone can, but after two months, we were still putting our best foot forward. We hadn't even had a real fight yet. How could you put your whole livelihood in the hands of somebody after knowing them for less than two months?

You certainly could do something like the TV show *Naked and Afraid* and just strip down, head into the wilderness, and see what happens. In the real world though, we need more time to hang out with each other and experience some different scenarios together. A questionnaire will only get you so far, especially when people are trying to put their best foot forward.

WHEN DISASTER STRIKES

I want to go back to my friends at Tempered Chocolate mentioned in Chapter 4. As you'll recall, Staci and Dan first opened 312 Pizza before expanding into the chocolate business. When they first decided to open the chocolate shop, it was an almost spontaneous decision. It had long been a dream of Staci's, and the perfect space suddenly became available. They had to jump on it right away or lose it. So even though 312 Pizza had only been open for six months, they decided to go ahead with developing the new business, signing the lease, and bringing in third-party financing.

They had one problem: They didn't actually know how to make chocolate. Luckily, they had recently become friends with a young lady who had studied at Le Cordon Bleu and had a background in chocolate. She was also from Chicago. Although they hadn't known her very long, Staci and Dan invited her to be the head chocolatier at Tempered and to have equity in the business.

This was a massive mistake.

The moment the business opened, it was like the new partner flipped a switch. She suddenly became extremely controlling and discouraged them from visiting the store. She would tell the employees she was the boss and Staci and Dan were just financial backers. She would call in and say she had decided to work from home—but how does the chocolate maker work from home? She brought in friends and gave them free wine, cheese, and chocolate.

She would give press interviews without running it past her business partners and would frequently go off message.

"It was almost like this weird competition I wasn't participating in," says Staci. "I was sales and marketing, so I'm the one that generally would set up interviews and craft the message that I want to go out to the public. Then I find out she's giving these interviewers full chef profiles for herself and her store with no mention of anybody else."

Staci struggled to balance the books, and the store started losing money. She knew she had a big problem. Eventually Staci and the chocolatier found themselves at my office in mediation because they just could not find any common ground for communication. In the end, they had to part ways. There was just no way to save the relationship.

What went wrong here? Everything, more or less. Mismatched expectations, lack of communication, financial issues—the works. Most importantly, Staci and Dan didn't really know the person they were getting into business with: She did a complete 180 and hijacked their dream.

GETTING BACK ON TRACK

A lot of people just suffer because they don't know what options are out there to try to fix their problems. They trek along in this stressed-out state indefinitely.

Do you know what happens when you ignore your relationship problems? They don't go away. Instead you suffer and your business suffers. Just like a child would suffer emotionally from seeing their parents in a terrible relationship, your business can't reach its full potential if its partners aren't able to work together to help it.

How do we turn this ship around?

GOING FOR COUNSELING

Sometimes, you really need outside help to get a better perspective and handle on your problems. When this happens in a marriage, you could see a therapist. In a business, you have other options.

If your relationship has gotten to the point where you are not able to have a conversation on your own and where you can only speak to each other via text and email, then it's time to bring in professional help. Admitting it's time to go see somebody is half the battle, but who do you see?

Business coaches are a fantastic option. Their role is to help you formulate a business plan and help you work through crucial decisions, but many can also help guide you and your partner through exercises to help you work out your issues.

Small business associations and entrepreneur centers can also help with conflict resolution.

If you need a more formal process, then consider seeing

a mediator or going to arbitration. Mediators are usually licensed attorneys who are trained to help resolve conflicts. A mediator is not a decision maker; they help the parties hash out their issues and maybe come to a resolution. Arbitration involves an individual who hears both sides of the issue and then renders a decision. The parties decide whether or not they want to be bound by the decision of an arbitrator.

We will discuss the process of mediation and arbitration more in depth in Chapter 7.

REVISITING THE CONTRACT

There is a reason we put so much effort into creating a comprehensive partnership agreement. This is your handbook to help you navigate many possible situations.

If you feel like one of you isn't fulfilling their designated responsibilities, you can pull out the agreement as a way to review your roles. It might be as simple as saying, "We agreed I was going to do this, and you were going to do that."

It can be used to provide guidance in an unexpected situation. For example, when Staci's father died, the operating agreement told us exactly how to handle that and what would happen to his LLC interest. It was a sad and stressful time, but we knew exactly what needed to happen next.

It can also be a tiebreaker if you are having a disagreement over how the business is supposed to run. No need for back and forth, just pull the agreement out and read it.

KEEP THE ROMANCE ALIVE

If you're starting to feel some tension with your partner, then you can try to head off any arguments by preemptively strengthening your relationship.

My husband and I try to find time to do fun things together. Sometimes I think we get bogged down in the grind of the everyday. Every day we get up, go to work, take care of the kid—all that stuff. You've really got to have some fun every now and then.

I think that is true for partners, individually and together. Find something to do that you both enjoy. In our case we tried ballroom dancing, but I couldn't stop trying to lead, and it frustrated the hell out of him. We settled on hang gliding as something we love to do together.

DON'T FREAK OUT

You don't need to abandon ship at the first sign of trouble. Don't say, "We've had a fight, it's all over, we're done." I think everybody owes it to each other and their business to give it the old college try.

The important thing is to identify conflicts early on. You may not realize how big a problem you have until it starts affecting the bottom line.

CHAPTER 6

THE AFFAIR

———

Friday nights were busy, but Monday afternoons at Twist were slow, slow, slow. Lance leaned on the bar and thought about fixing himself a gin and tonic. For once, Larissa wasn't around to nag him about it.

Lately, she had been on his case about every little thing. He needed to help more, he needed to drink less, he needed to finish paperwork faster, on and on and on. In his heart, Lance felt like he was trying his best, but the restaurant business was so new to him and sometimes it was hard to keep up with everything that was going on.

On the other hand, he had to admit that owning a bar was great. Twist was doing well, several local newspapers had written favorable reviews, and there was a healthy buzz going around. Even better, he felt like the most popular guy in town every night and was meeting all sorts of interesting people.

Just last night, he'd met a fascinating woman named Marissa who was thinking about starting her own bar down the street. The idea was very hot and trendy: alcoholic milkshakes.

"Think about it," she'd said. "People *love* ice cream. People *love* cocktails. It's the perfect union."

Lance thought it was brilliant. Marissa was brilliant. Quite pretty too, with dark hair and long lashes.

After a couple of drinks at the bar, she had leaned in and flirtatiously whispered, "You know, you should think about going in with me. You've done such a great job on this place, and I could use a guy with a head for business."

It was a very enticing offer. He told her he'd think it over, but now he has the urge to call her and accept. After all, he's a free man. He can do whatever he wants.

Larissa can just deal with it.

WANDERING EYE SYNDROME

Sometimes when things aren't going well with a business, one of the partners gets a wandering eye. They think they can shake things up and improve their situation with or without the consent of their business partner.

I find that affairs in a business relationship can take one of two forms. The first is someone trying to bring in a new business partner to the existing arrangement. The second scenario is

one of the partners dividing their attention by jumping into a new business venture, like our friend Lance.

Neither of these is necessarily a death sentence for your relationship if everything is done on the up and up. Many people can and do make these new scenarios work, but there are certain things you need to keep in mind.

BRINGING IN NEW BLOOD

When a business ends up strapped for cash, one or both partners might want to bring in a third-party investor to join their union.

This is another tricky situation that must be navigated carefully. Finding the right special someone can be tough because you are adding another element—another personality—into a partnership that might already be sinking. I've seen horror stories where investors are brought in to contribute money, but instead they swoop in and want to control all the decisions and alter the dynamics of the business.

Don't part with equity for anything but money. You sometimes see situations where a new partner isn't contributing money, but instead contributes new connections or sweat equity. If they don't follow through, you've given away some of your equity for nothing. I despise this kind of stupidity. At the end of the day, your business needs money to run.

Investors are supposed to be giving you money. Investors who promise introductions and intangible fluffy things are not the ones you want or need. Unless that person can literally call Bill Gates on the phone right now and Bill Gates says, "I'll give you whatever you want," it's not worth it. Money talks better than promises.

It's amazing how quickly many of these "investors" disappear when you ask them to pony up some money. If you're not willing to put your money where your mouth is, don't be an entrepreneur.

A MARRIAGE OF CONVENIENCE

The family from 312 Pizza and Tempered have an excellent relationship with an investor who helps keep their business running. I reached out to Staci to find out why their setup works so well.

When the family first started 312, they were using money from their parent's retirement fund as well as investments from other family members. When one family member pulled out, they had a huge hole in their budget. They met with one investor who was willing to contribute the money they needed but wanted a controlling interest in the company. That didn't work for them, but they didn't have a lot of options.

Enter Cees Brinkman.

Cees is a delightful man from the Netherlands who invests in quite a few restaurants around Nashville. He was set up with Staci and Dan through mutual connections.

Cees invited the couple over for dinner one night. They didn't talk a single word about business. He simply wanted to see what kind of people they were. At the end of the night, he agreed to invest. This isn't necessarily the method of vetting your partner that I would recommend, but it worked out.

Cees is not just an investor; he's a mentor and a friend. Although he doesn't have official decision-making power in the business, they often turn to him for his years of expertise.

"We definitely use him as a resource because he's got such a great vision for things. That helps keep the relationship trustworthy. He's not just the money. We definitely value his opinion."

INVESTORS GONE WILD

Not every investor story has a happy ending. Sometimes bringing someone else into the company can be a complete and utter disaster.

Allison had a burgeoning textile business but didn't have the overhead to expand fast enough to meet the demands of her clients. She connected with a local investor named Jerry who agreed to invest the money she needed to start a micro-mill with an industrial loom, studio space, and several employees.

Allison and her husband Roger contacted a lawyer (not me) and wrote up a contract. Things started to get lopsided right away when Jerry insisted on 51 percent ownership of the company to their 49 percent. They agreed that once his loan to the company was repaid, they would revert to 50/50 ownership. Allison really needed the money, so they agreed with the provision that they could buy themselves out of the contract if things went south.

They signed their contract and found a large space to set up shop. Immediately things started to get weird. Allison and Roger believed that Jerry would help with the financials but that Allison would be in charge of running the business. Instead, Jerry started spending all day, every day at the work space. He badgered Allison constantly with questions and grumbled over every expense. Sometimes he would simply hover over Allison and the employees, watching.

Eventually, they started to see a more volatile side of his personality. He would get in heated arguments with Allison and would disparage her in front of business associates. He alienated important clients with his comments.

When Jerry's initial investment ran out, Allison and Roger decided it was time to cut their losses. They went to mediation and made a plan to dissolve the business and pay Jerry back. Then they discovered Jerry's bookkeeping was totally inaccurate and ended up in a long, drawn-out legal battle over what was owed.

What complicated things, and perhaps explains his reluctance to spend money, was that he personally had to take out a loan for $50,000 to contribute the capital he had promised. Yes, he didn't even own the money he intended to invest. The fact that he couldn't provide the money he committed to up front should have been a huge red flag.

VETTING A NEW INVESTOR

You've made the leap and want to bring a third party into your cozy relationship. Now what?

You shouldn't take money from just anyone. Do your research on this new person. We need to know about their financial situation and what other businesses they have invested in. Are they accredited?

Here are some questions to get you started on your due diligence for a potential investor:

1. Ask about past investing activity. Is this their first investment, or have they invested in other ventures? If the former, you will want to ask about why they are choosing to invest in the venture. What do they hope to get out of the investment? If the latter, you will want to know about the past ventures and you will absolutely want to speak to those individuals about their experience with the investor.

2. What are their goals for their investment? Obviously, they would like a favorable ROI. Do they see themselves having a passive role or an active role in the business?
3. Be sure whatever capital they are investing is readily available and know where the money is coming from.

MOONLIGHTING

Some people are addicted to the rush of a new relationship. It's heady and exciting and far more stimulating than the day-to-day slog of actually running a business.

Not so fast, though! You can't run around starting new businesses if it might damage your original enterprise. When you own a business, you have certain legal duties to it such as fiduciary duties and duties of good faith, loyalty, and fair dealing. This is true in almost every jurisdiction.

Fiduciary duty means you can't steal from your business. The duty of good faith, loyalty, and fair dealing means you're going to do the right thing by your business. It doesn't have to be your one and only, but you should make decisions that benefit it, and you can't do anything to purposely harm it.

Lance's plan to open what was essentially a competing

bar down the street from his original business could back-fire on him badly. If you do things to purposely damage your business, that opens you up to lawsuits from your partners or from the business itself. Yes, that's right, the baby business can sue the mommy and daddy. They can, and they do.

It's very common among feuding partners for one to claim the other has breached their duties because they've done something competitive. If Lance were to go open a bar down the street from Twist, I would argue that could be a breach of good faith and fair dealing with his first business. If Business B does well, it's going to take away business from the original bar—and that is a problem.

Even worse would be if Lance started taking money out of the till to buy a fryer for the new business, or if he started poaching employees to come work for his new business. You should not do these things, or it could end very, very badly for you.

MAKING AN OPEN RELATIONSHIP WORK

Being involved in more than one business, or having multiple business partners isn't inherently a bad thing. In fact, it's a situation where some entrepreneurs thrive.

Take my client Mark Rubin, who owns half a dozen franchises of 1-800-GOT-JUNK spread across the country. He has active partnerships in Nashville, Raleigh, Brooklyn, and several other cities. With each one, there are at least four people that own each franchise—three of whom are consistently the same and who sometimes bring in someone different.

Dealing with one partnership is hard; doing six is like, holy cow! But he's learned how to be with many different businesses successfully.

One of the reasons he is successful at keeping so many balls in the air is that he does his due diligence before investing in each new venture.

"I am good at keeping my feelers out there," Mark said. "People in the junk system know I'm always in acquisition mode, so I get wind of deals early. Then I run some numbers, and if the numbers look good, I bring them to the other guys."

Mark told me he knows very well what his own strengths are and what his partners' are. He does his thing and he gets out of their way, and they do the same. I think that is what makes them work so well together.

Now that Mark's portfolio is so large, he's making some

changes to his business model, like moving towards aggregating his business interests. He's found that it is easier to bring people together than to keep each company separate.

"We're going to rent a fabulous house somewhere and have all the managers meet. It's very hard to run these remote operations in an efficient way because we're not there. We're trying to come up with a way to consolidate our holdings and really operate it like a portfolio of companies rather than a series of individual companies."

CH-CH-CHANGES

Businesses change over time. Sometimes a partnership needs to evolve along with it. What's important is to make sure you are always putting the interests and integrity of your business first.

CHAPTER 7

MARRIAGE COUNSELING

It was a quiet Monday evening when I stopped by Twist for a quick after-work drink. I visit all my client's establishments on a regular basis, partly to check in and partly because most of them have awesome businesses.

When there is a lot of tension in a business, you can often feel it as soon as you enter the room. Negative energy hung like a cloud over the bar.

I spotted Larissa and hailed her over, "Hey, what's going on? The place looks great!"

One look at her face told me all I needed to know: Things were not going well at all.

"Here, let's sit down and have some drinks. Tell me what's going on."

It didn't take much to get her to spill. Things with Lance had reached an impasse. They weren't even speaking to each other, communicating only through the waitstaff and terse emails. Tension carried over to their employees, and even the clientele were picking up on the stressful vibe. Sales were slipping. Larissa dreaded coming into work each day.

"This used to be fun, but now I'm just exhausted," Larissa said, wiping her eyes.

I'd seen this plenty of times before, and I knew the only remedy was to get everyone in a room and have it out.

"Look, you know what?" I told her, "Why don't I reach out to both you and Lance and schedule a time for you guys to come in, and we can talk it through? I think you need to hash this out before this goes from bad to worse."

"I'm not sure he'll agree to that."

I had heard this before, too. "If you ask him to, he won't. If I ask him to, I bet he will. You'll see."

ADMITTING YOU NEED HELP

More than once, I've gotten the panicky call from a client telling me things have gone south in their relationship. The business is in shambles because they can't even be in the same room together. Their marriage is failing.

Luckily, a good partnership agreement already holds the key to your salvation. We usually put in something called a "deadlock provision." If you are stuck in a situation where the business can't function anymore because of conflicts for a certain period of time, that is considered a deadlock, which triggers certain events. Usually after thirty days of deadlock, both partners agree to go into mediation.

This is a great thing to build in to your agreement because the decision is already made for you ahead of time, and you don't have to argue over it when all the chips are on the table. You basically go into autopilot.

If one of the partners calls me, distressed because their business is in a death spiral and they only have enough money left to pay one more month's rent, I usually bring up the partnership agreement, and off to counseling we go.

WHAT MEDIATION IS (AND ISN'T)

Oftentimes, people don't really understand what mediation entails. It's important to understand the difference between mediation and arbitration.

Mediation is when all parties have agreed to come together with a licensed mediator to try to work out their differences and perhaps come to an agreement on what to do. The mediator has no legal power whatsoever when it comes to making a decision; they are simply there to help move the conversation forward.

Arbitration is completely different. If the parties have stipulated they are going to binding arbitration, it's a lot like what you see on *Judge Judy*. Here's a fun fact: Most TV judges are actually arbitrators. You agree to go before a person (not an actual judge) in a court-like setting. Usually there are opening statements, arguments, evidence, the whole thing. Then the arbitrator decides. If you've subjected yourself to binding arbitration, then you have agreed to accept whatever decision the arbitrator comes down with. If you have not agreed to be bound, then it would be considered nonbinding arbitration, and you don't have to accept it until after you hear the decision.

Some agreements state you must go to mediation, and if you can't come to a decision together, you must then go to arbitration. Some agreements send you straight to arbitration. It really depends on the situation.

The reason we do these things is that mediation and arbitration are typically much cheaper and faster options than having to go to court to settle differences.

WHAT TO EXPECT

The goal of mediation is to find a path forward.

I'm a big fan of mediation because it's an excellent way to push over a difficult hump. It offers a structured environment with a neutral third party who has the skills to unpack your issues and help you decide how to move forward. It may not be the decision you want, but at least you won't be deadlocked any longer.

Mediation practices vary depending on the facilitator and how contentious things are, but they usually follow a similar format. Parties start out in the same room, we lay down some ground rules, and usually both sides get to give a little opening statement.

After that, the two parties will often split into separate rooms so they can speak openly and freely to the mediator. One of the ground rules is that the mediator will only relay to the other side what you want them to tell them; anything else they have to keep confidential. Then the mediator will spend some time with the other party, figuring out what they want. Afterwards, the mediator tries to negotiate an agreement between the parties.

A common issue in business relationships is that one partner doesn't feel they are being heard by the other. In that situation, the mediator holds everyone to the rules so everyone can say their piece.

Sometimes you can find an easy fix to your problem. Sometimes you really cannot. You just dive in and see.

Here is an example of how I've used mediation to help a struggling business.

TEMPERED CHOCOLATE

I'm not a licensed mediator, but I have the right training as an attorney to provide these services if needed. I acted as such when Staci, Dan, and their renegade chocolate maker from Chapter 5 came to see me. We were convinced the only way to confront their power struggle issues was to do it head on.

During mediation, it quickly became clear that we were dealing with two fundamentally different views of reality. The chocolatier was very young and inexperienced with the business world. She believed Tempered was her business and Staci and Dan were simply fronting the money as silent partners.

That was not what they intended or wanted for their business. The idea was always Staci's. She had found the space, created the business plan, and imagined the concept before the chocolatier was ever in the picture.

Things did not go smoothly in mediation. It almost felt like the chocolatier was a small child having a tantrum. The ugliness came out. At one point, Staci had to excuse herself because she was so upset.

After six hours of sitting in a room, trying to figure it out, it became very clear they were not going to be able to continue working together. They needed to part ways. There was no other way for them to get past their differences, so splitting up was the right decision.

Staci and Dan decided to buy the chocolatier out of the business.

That seems like a bad result, but it actually turned out to be a happy ending. Staci immediately enrolled in chocolate making classes and learned how to run the business on her own. Now Tempered is thriving, making money, and creating fantastic chocolate.

FINDING A MEDIATOR

Finding a mediator or arbitrator is simple. The American Arbitration Association, or as we like to call it, the AAA, is a good place to start. Their website is www.ADR.org. If you have no background experience with mediation or arbitration, this is the easiest way to get the ball moving.

On the website, you submit a statement of your case and pay a fee. Once you file a case with them, they will guide you through the process of conflict resolution quite quickly. They will help you find a licensed mediator (or arbitrator), set a date, and complete your mediation. Some situations, like conflicts in the construction or the entertainment industry, require specialized mediators. You may have to wait for one to become available.

You can also simply conduct a web search for "mediators" and your town. Chances are, quite a few options will pop right up. Another option is to contact your state bar association. Both of these options are potentially more economical than using the AAA, but it will most likely take a bit longer to schedule a consultation, which can be a drawback if you have a problem that needs a quick resolution.

YOU DON'T HAVE TO SUFFER

Nobody wants to go to counseling. But if you keep letting the elephant in the room get bigger and bigger and bigger, sooner or later the elephant is going to be the only thing left in the room. It will crush everything else.

If the tensions in your relationship have escalated to the point where you can't figure out how to move forward, it's time to get outside help. A mediator can help you communicate more effectively and can potentially save your business.

CHAPTER 8

DIVORCE

The birds were chirping, the sun was shining, and Lance was lying in bed, feeling miserable.

He knew he needed to get up, get dressed, and head in to work for the staff meeting, but he just couldn't seem to pull himself out of bed. He could blame the pounding in his head on the shots he took last night, but that still didn't explain the dread in his heart.

When Twist first opened, it seemed like the culmination of all his dreams, but now every day felt stressed and tense. He'd tried to work through mediation with Larissa, but it felt like they were speaking two different languages.

On the flip side, things at Milk Bar were shaping up great. Marissa was just so fun to work with and the concept was so new and fresh. Alcoholic milkshakes were about to be the Next Big Thing. He found himself spending more and more time there and less and less time at Twist. Then he felt guilty.

He was stretching himself too thin. It felt like he was lying in bed with his wife but thinking about his mistress. It wasn't fair to him, he realized. It wasn't fair to any of them. Milk Bar was the one. He needed to be there for it full time.

He felt terrible leaving Larissa in the lurch, but she would probably be better off in the long run. He'd done his best and it was time to cut his losses and stop the bleeding.

Lance sighed and looked at the clock. He picked up the phone and dialed a familiar number, "Rachel, it's Lance. I can't do this anymore."

KNOWING WHEN TO CALL IT QUITS

This is how it usually happens: Somebody calls me crying at seven in the morning. Something has broken the camel's back. Usually it's something small and seemingly insignificant, but it's the last straw and this partner wants out.

While I believe it's important to go through steps like mediation to try to salvage the situation, there can come a point where you have to say, "We need to be done working with each other and move on."

How do you know when you've reached that point? When your relationship is killing your business. If your business is bleeding money, if it's unable to grow and flourish. If you and your partner cannot come together and make healthy decisions for the business. If the owners are at each other's throats or completely not speaking. These are all signs that you need to consider parting ways.

Sometimes, the law might make the decision for you. It's like having a child. If you're not feeding it and you're not caring for it, then guess what? The state is going to come and take it away. If you aren't making good decisions for your business, then the statute or your partnership agreement may push you to dissolve or sell the business. It's in the public's interest not to have a bunch of businesses sitting around doing nothing.

At this point, I have to remind the partners that I represent the child in their divorce. I am there on behalf of the business. The first thing I need to figure out is if this is going to be an amicable split or a contested one.

Generally, there are three different roads a business divorce can take: Dissolution, Contention, or a Buy/Sell situation.

A VERY MESSY BREAKUP

Let's talk about what happens when a breakup goes very, very badly. This example doesn't involve a client of mine; it's the sad case of Manny Randazzo King Cakes.

Manny and Dianne Randazzo were a married couple who ran a business in New Orleans called Manny Randazzo King Cakes. Randazzo's makes, without a doubt, the best king cake in the world. During Mardi Gras, the line stretches around the block to get in, and you see people leaving with twenty cakes at a time. It's that wonderful.

It was a family business. Manny's father had done it before him, and his kids grew up in the store. Manny and Dianne opened their bakery in 1992. Dianne worked the counter, and Manny ran the ovens in the back.

What happened next was a bad marital breakup *and* a bad business divorce. They split, Manny kept the bakery, and Dianne got almost a million dollars for her piece of the company. She didn't sign a noncompete agreement, and there were no legal restraints put in place to keep her from starting her own bakery. Great for her, not so great for him.

So, what does Dianne do? She turns right around and sets up her own bakery called Dianne Randazzo Bakery, selling, you guessed it, king cakes. I don't know what went on in their marriage, but that is some revenge baking.

They built a business together, they got divorced, she opened a competing business with almost the same name, and in the end, everyone ended up in court.

Ultimately Manny got an injunction, and the name was changed, but that was a very expensive, very unpleasant experience for everyone. Manny had to spend a ton of money on lawyers and court fees. It all could have been avoided if their original dissolution agreement had contained the right language—and maybe if Manny had been nicer to his wife.

UNTIL DISSOLUTION DO US PART

Dissolution happens when both parties come together and say, "We're done. We don't want to do this anymore. We just want to liquidate and go our separate ways." In this situation, neither partner wants to run the business and they can't find a qualified buyer who wants to purchase the business and take over.

Most of the time, your partnership agreement will stipulate how to dissolve your business. If you don't have a partnership agreement, then your state's governing statues can guide you in how it works. In most jurisdictions, this process is called winding up the business.

If you're going to dissolve a business, then the first thing you have to do is collect all the physical assets of the business and prepare to sell them off.

After you sell everything off, you'll have a chunk of money. Don't start divvying it up yet. First, you need to pay your outside creditors—people like banks, vendors, and landlords. They always get the first bite of the apple. Then the internal creditors get their share. If one of the owners has lent money to the business via a promissory note, that money should be repaid next.

If there's anything left, then the owners of the company would split it based on their share of equity. So, if one person had 60 percent equity, they would get 60 percent of what's left over, and so on.

What if there isn't enough money to fulfill all these obligations? Then you have to work something out with your creditors. They could try suing the LLC, but if all the assets have already been liquidated, they might just be out of luck. If your business is an incorporated entity (hopefully it is), the owners themselves shouldn't be liable for any of that business debt.

If you didn't incorporate despite my warnings in Chapter 3, then any leftover debt will fall onto the partners. This is again based on your equity split. If you own 80 percent of the company, you will be responsible for 80 percent of the debt. If you don't have an agreement, the law presumes you are 50/50 whether you like it or not.

If you've loaned money to the business and there isn't enough to pay you back, you are also probably out of luck unless you decide to go after your partner for that money in court, which could be very, very, messy and expensive.

Some businesses aren't worth anything because they're mired in debt. That's where a lot of people get their panties in a wad, protesting, "I own 50 percent of this company!" Yes, you own 50 percent of a ship that's sinking. If you want it, then by all means, help yourself!

Finally, there are some corporate details to be cleaned up. Usually, you file final tax returns, file dissolution and termination paperwork with the Secretary of State, and then you go on your merry way. You're done.

GIVING UP CUSTODY: BUY/SELL

If one partner wants to exit the company and one wants to stay, then the remaining partner will need to buy the other one out. If the departing partner leaves willingly, this is a straightforward process. If not...well, then skip down to the next section.

You must buy your partner's share of the business, and that's going to be a substantial cost depending on how much equity they have and how much your company is worth. If you've got the money and the desire to get out, it should be a no-brainer. But if you don't have the money, that's where things get very difficult and you find yourself in a bit of a stalemate.

A lot of businesses don't plan for that exit. Where is the money going to come to from? This can be a big issue and is a reason a lot of partners stay together far longer than they should. They simply can't afford to buy out the other person.

Like a couple that stays married solely for financial reasons, nobody is going to be very happy stuck in a situation like this.

The partner wishing to continue running the business can look into getting a small business loan to fund the buyout, but that can be tricky. Most banks want to lend to a business for a profit-driven reason. Funding a buyout is not typically considered a profit-generating activity and is, more often than not, an indication of trouble within the business.

Another option is seller financing—i.e., your (soon to be) former partner agrees to allow you to sign a promissory note to pay them the price for their share over time. This scenario has many issues. Once you sign a promissory note, you are most likely personally liable for paying your former partner the price, and title to their interest does not pass until you pay the note in full, plus interest. If you default, your former partner can accelerate the debt and sue you for the entire balance.

One forward-thinking idea would be for the partners to agree to open a bank account as an emergency fund. This could be used for emergency situations, or for a potential buyout in the future. You would absolutely want to memorialize the existence of this fund in the partnership agreement and what it is to be used for, but think of it like saving for a rainy day.

Incidentally, there is a similar product called key man insurance that acts as a kind of life insurance on the partners in a business. If something were to happen to one of the partners (e.g., one of you were to die or become incapacitated), you get the money to fill their role with a salaried person. You have a life insurance policy on your spouse—why not on your partner?

WHEN THINGS GET UGLY

What if you're done working with your business partner, but they don't want to leave? What if you both want to keep the business?

A lot of people don't understand that you can't just remove an owner from your company. If they have equity, you can't just kick them out. Owning equity is like owning property. It may be intangible, but it can't be taken away from you without an exchange of something of value.

Even if you had a majority interest in the company, you can't just expel another member. You could take away their voting rights, but they will always have a financial interest in the company unless you buy them out. If you were doing something fraudulent with your company such as stealing, you could be expelled as a voting rights owner of the organization, but you would still have the financial interest.

When I write partnership agreements, I usually include

parameters on when you can take someone's decision-making powers away and possibly trigger a forced buyout. Even in this situation, you're still going to have to square up with them on money.

If things get contentious and we can't reach some sort of agreement among ourselves, then we go to court. If we can't agree on the valuation for the business, if we can't agree on who keeps the business, if we have tried everything and can't find common ground, then it's time to have a judge or possibly an arbitrator figure it out.

We want to avoid this if possible because it's expensive and it takes a long time. Litigation is always about splitting the baby. You're going to come out with either the top or bottom half of a baby, which means at the end of the day, you're still going to have a dead baby. Nobody is going to be super happy about that.

A GOOD DIVORCE

It's not all terrible. Splits can happen amicably. Sometimes after all the drama is done, everyone simply agrees things aren't working and need to end. It's still painful, but it's easier.

One pair of my clients met when they were working

together at a middle school and bonded over their love of beer. Partner A wanted to start his own brewery and asked Partner B to join him. Partner A had the beer knowledge and Partner B had the business know-how. After a few fits and starts, they opened their brewery.

Right off the bat, these two guys made several mistakes: They didn't clearly define their roles, and they didn't have super compatible personalities. Everything went fine in the honeymoon phase, but once they started having financial difficulties and other stressors, the shit hit the fan.

Their relationship deteriorated to the point where Partner B felt things were unworkable. They couldn't find a healthy way to communicate and were in a deadlock.

Partner B tells me, "I was increasingly vocal about opposing some of Partner A's ideas and opinions. I could have done it much better I'm sure, but I was tired and stressed. In the end, anything I said, Partner A would just automatically argue against."

He told Partner A they should plan for Partner B to transition out over the next six months. In response, Partner A told him that if he had one foot out the door he should probably just leave now. This told Partner B that Partner A was ready for him to leave anyway.

So, Partner B left as amicably as these things can go. Partner A continued with the business. Their business relationship is dead, but they've remained relatively cordial socially, which is about the best you can hope for in a situation like this.

When I asked Partner B what he would do differently the next time around, he told me, "Lay down some ground rules and some boundaries. And I think for us the biggest thing is that I wish I would have communicated my business ethos and philosophy of how a business should run on a more grounded level and communicated it better."

HOPE FOR THE BEST, PLAN FOR THE WORST

If I could stress one thing in this chapter, it's the importance of planning ahead. You should talk about buy/sell scenarios and partnership agreement provisions at the very beginning. I literally bring it up with every single one of my clients. We want to do this while everyone is hunky dory and happy.

Nobody wants to think about the possibility of splitting up down the road, but look: Nothing lasts forever. You're happy now, but at some point, things may change, and we need to be prepared for that. We want to plan for the possibility of a split just as much as we plan for success.

CHAPTER 9

MAKE-UP SEX

—

Larissa sipped her Diet Coke and checked her watch. Panera was buzzing with the usual Saturday afternoon entrepreneur crowd, and she zealously guarded her table while she waited for her three o'clock appointment to arrive.

"Larissa? Hey!"

Larissa turned to see Lance standing in the aisle. Her heart did a little flip-flop. It had been almost a year since they'd gone their separate ways. At first, she'd been avoiding him, but then she forgot about him a little bit. Business was thriving, and there just wasn't time to dwell on past mistakes.

"Hiya, Lance. How are you? You look great!" He really did. He'd lost weight, and some of the puffiness around his eyes had dissipated.

"Yeah, I quit drinking a few months ago. Been great for the ol' waistline." He paused awkwardly. "I guess you heard about what happened with Milk Bar?"

Larissa nodded. The place had opened big, then gone out of business within two months. It sounded like a total disaster.

"Yeah...apparently ice cream and cocktails weren't a good mix. They just made people feel drunk and gassy. Who could have guessed? But hey, it seems like Twist is doing fantastic!"

They chatted a bit back and forth, and it almost felt like the old days. Larissa told him about their expansion and her plans for a second location. She was just meeting with potential investors now and locking down the rest of the funding.

"It's funny," said Lance, "I'm actually here to vet a new business partner as well. I'm still chasing the dream I guess." There was a long pause. "You know, this sounds crazy but...would you show me your business plan? Maybe we could give it another go?"

Larissa paused. Her eyes met Lance's. She'd have to think about that one.

PROCEED (WITH CAUTION)

We started this book with the story of my Mom's disastrous business divorce. It was a cautionary tale, but not a tragic one. At the end of the day, she survived. More than that, she took the lessons she learned after ten years in the database business and started a new company that is now extremely successful.

A bad relationship isn't going to kill you. A lot of people feel like a failure if their business doesn't work out. At the end of the day, divorce doesn't have to equal failure. It might just be the best thing for the business and for you.

If you've read this far, you might be starting to feel a bit antsy. There is a lot to think about when entering a business relationship and a lot of potential pitfalls. My goal wasn't to scare everyone half to death about the things that can go wrong when starting a business, although fear is a powerful tool for an attorney. The biggest thing I want people to take away from this book is that your business goals are achievable, if you choose the right partner. I want to stress the importance of doing your due diligence to make your relationship work so you can go on to do great things.

In that vein, I want to share some examples from my clients with great business relationships that are working well, and why.

EAST NASHVILLE BEER WORKS

Anthony and Sean are an interesting case in that I wouldn't necessarily have pegged them for success.

Anthony knew he liked craft beer and felt like he could sell the heck out of it, but he had no idea how to make it. So, he put out an open call on Facebook looking for a business partner. Really, he did that.

That's how he ended up with Sean, who was a friend of a friend. Sean basically lives, eats, and breathes craft beer. I'm pretty sure he sleeps inside a fermenter in his apartment.

They went into a business arrangement that always gives me pause: Anthony and outside investors were providing all the money, and Sean was strictly bringing sweat equity. In my experience, partnerships where this is the setup tend not to survive because the expectations are usually not well aligned.

Not so with Anthony and Sean. If there were a picture in the dictionary next to "sweat equity," that picture would be of Sean. Sean proves himself every day and continually earns the right to be an owner of the brewery.

That's one reason their partnership works, but Anthony told me the other: communication.

"We do a lot of huddles," Anthony says. They have a standing meeting every week with just the two of them and the bar manager, then frequent one-on-ones. Although technically Anthony has 80 percent equity to Sean's 20 percent regarding governance rights, they make decisions as democratically as possible. They trust each other.

If I had looked at them when they first started, I probably would have bet money on them not making it, but they're about to complete their first year, and it looks like they have really found a great match with each other.

THE POST EAST

You remember Chris and Tonya from way back in Chapter 1? The couple who tackled marriage and a business partnership all in one summer?

The Post East coffee shop thrives despite existing in a

very crowded niche. They are leading the pack when it comes to vegan and gluten-free dining in Nashville. Their coffee shop is a part of the community and is a resource center, with Tonya as the face of the business who brings people together in her shop. So how do they keep both relationships running smoothly? Massive amounts of communication.

Tonya says, "You can't expect the person that you're in partnership with to know what's going on in your head. You have to make sure that you're communicating concerns, thoughts, and ideas to them. A lot of times, it's through omission of information rather than just misunderstanding of information that leads to conflict in that partnership."

Additionally, she speaks of the importance of compromise. Businesses change constantly, and it's important to be able to adapt, change your expectations, and to be willing to let go of things that aren't working. Tonya is the dreamer and Chris is the realist. Together, their ideas even out. Their bond is so strong in part because of their romantic relationship.

Tonya says, "I think the times when we want to walk away and throw our hands up, the other person is there. I'm there for him, or he's there to remind me we're in this together and are here to support each other. We may not have all the answers, but eventually, things will make sense and we'll figure it out together."

312 PIZZA COMPANY

Then there are my old favorites, the family behind 312 Pizza and Tempered Chocolate.

These guys have gone through so much. The death of Staci's father, Dan's battle with stage 3 colon cancer, the fallout from the conflict at Tempered—and they've only been in business for three years! Any one of those things might have crumbled a lesser union.

But they keep rising up every time. It's like nothing can tear them down. I think they have the greatest connection between them, as a family and as a business. They have such a solid foundation of communication and work experience. It's a testament to their drive, their perseverance, their determination, their stubbornness—all these great entrepreneurial traits.

They are stronger together than they would be if any one of them tried to go at this individually. It's real proof that two (or five) heads can be better than one. They just keep thriving. They are about to open their second 312 and are looking to open a third out of state. It's a real display of how a partnership can be fruitful and beneficial for everyone involved.

TREAT YOUR BUSINESS PARTNER LIKE YOUR MOST IMPORTANT RELATIONSHIP

I make all my new clients go through an extended version of my business questionnaire from Chapter 1. I think a lot of them roll their eyes and do it to humor me, but I wonder sometimes, "If my mom and her business partner had gone through these steps, would the results have been different?" I think she still would have gone into business with her partner, but maybe the dissolution would have been less stressful and more beneficial for both partners.

If this book saves just one partnership or even prevents someone from going into an unfit partnership, I will feel like I have done my job.

Most people do not meet someone, get married, and have a kid in a two-month time span. More often people meet each other, date, go through conflicts, resolve conflicts, go through more conflicts. They work on their relationships every day if they want to have successful, long-term marriages.

When you start a business with someone, you are business-marrying them. You are entwining your lives, livelihoods, and incomes. You need to treat it with the same amount of care and protection that you would a marital relationship.

There is no one right way to make things work, but you do need to have a plan. Remember: those who fail to plan, plan to fail. It's up to you what side of the statistics you want to be on.

ACKNOWLEDGEMENTS

So many people to thank! First of all, this book would not have happened without Book in A Box. Thank you to Trey Meyers for introducing me to this wonderful company. Thanks to my editorial team Dan Bernitt, Holly Hudson, Stephanie Yoder, and of course, the infamous Tucker Max for seeing the potential in this book and for keeping me on track!

I want to thank all of my clients who took the time to share more of their stories with me: Staci and Dan Bockman, Anthony Davis and Sean Jewett, Chris and Tonya, Michael K., Roger Shelton, Kevin Lewis, the MacKenzies, and Mark Rubin. I also want to thank every single one of my clients, past and present. The inspiration for this book comes from all of you, and this book is for all of you! Thank you for giving me the honor of representing you. You have made my life pursuit of the practice of law truly wonderful.

I want to thank my Schaffer Law Firm family. Kelcy, you are one of the best things that has ever happened to me in business and in life! Thank you for taking a chance on the firm and on me, for doing a tremendous job every day, and for taking my balls away when I need it! To my interns Sam, Landon, and Julianne, thanks for bringing your energy and talent to my office and for putting up with my crazy!

I want to thank my beautiful family. To my extended families, the Schaffers, Lawsons, Beckhams and DeVaults, thank you for being supportive of me while going through this process. To the men in my life, my wonderful husband Tyler, my beautiful son Declan, and my devoted father Jeff, you are the most wonderful husband, son, and father a girl could ask for!

Finally, I want to give a very special thanks my mother, Pat. Mom, there are no words to describe how much you mean to me, how much I love you, and how much this book would not have happened without you. You are and continue to be the most inspirational person in my life. I have always loved and appreciated your strength, perseverance, and courage, but I don't think I really saw the big picture of all you have accomplished personally and professionally until we presented together at the mother-daughter coffee conversation at Pathways a few years ago. Hearing the story of how you began a career in the male-dominated industry of computing at a time when there were no personal computers and emerged as an expert in your field will stay with me forever. I also did not truly appreciate that you did all of this *and* raised me until Declan came into this world. You have set the example of what I aspire to be as an entrepreneur, as a woman, and as a mother. Thank you for being my mom. I love you so much!

ABOUT THE AUTHOR

**RACHEL SCHAFFER LAWSON**
knows small business because she's
a small business owner herself. In
March 2011, she launched Schaffer
Law Firm, PLLC, providing quality
legal services to innovative entrepreneurs, budding restaurateurs,
impactful nonprofits, and a wide
variety of arts and entertainment organizations. Rachel
graduated from Northeastern University, then went on to
study business and entertainment law at Loyola University
College of Law in New Orleans. She lives in Nashville,
Tennessee, with her husband, their young son, and a half-
dozen cats and dogs.

Made in the USA
Columbia, SC
21 March 2018